Angela De

MANAGER BY CHANCE

A Guide to Survival in Business

MORELLINI EDITORE

Copyright 2024 © Morellini Editore by Enzimi Srl

ENZIMI

Via Porro Lambertenghi 7
20159 Milano
www.morellinieditore.it
info@morellinieditore.it
facebook.com/morellinied
instagram.com/morellinieditore

Cover illustration: Sandro Crisafi
Graphic design: márGo
Translated by Christina Angelilli

ISBN: 979-12-5527-251-9

All rights reserved in accordance with the law and international conventions.

To young managers, so that they know that "young" and "manager" are contradictory terms even on Wikipedia. A manager gets old fast.
To experienced managers, to tell them that there is always a way to get out alive. If you have found it, write to me.
To real managers, with admiration.

Index

Foreword by Chance 7
Warnings 9
Introduction.............................. 11
Who Is a Manager 13
The Manager Population........ 15
The Climbing Manager 17
The Highlander Manager 20
The Cassandra Manager 23
The Pontius Pilate
Manager 27
The Manager in Love................ 29
The Incontinent Manager 33
The Penelope Manager 36
The Aging Manager 40
The Performance
Manager 43
The Dictator Manager 46
The Chanel Manager................ 54
The Nerdy Manager 58
The Willy Wonka Manager....... 62
The Vulcan Manager 65
The Geeky Manager 69
The Designer Manager 73
The Structured Manager.......... 76
The Enlightened Manager 80

Life as a Manager 83
A Leader Is not
Denied to Anyone 85
The Manager
and ~~Free~~ Time 89
The BOD Room 91
"Meetingitis Kills" 94
The Manager
Goes to School 101
The Manager's Tools 105
Manager Meets
Other Managers................. 107
The Manager
and the Consultant............ 110
The Manager
Goes to the Dance 113
The Manager
Reaps Victims 117
Pills 121
How to Survive 123
The Disciple....................... 135
The Manager Happens
to Be a Manager................. 137
And You, Which
Manager Are You?............. 138
Acknowledgements............. 143
Author 147

5

Foreword by Chance

I had the pleasure of hearing Angela Deganis speak in February 2024 in Milan, and she kindly gave me a copy of her book, in the original Italian version. Now, my Italian is ok, so I read parts of it, slowly but I read and enjoyed it. Unfortunately, one of the key words here are "slowly", so when she reached out to me and told me that it was being translated into English, and asked whether I would like to read it and give a foreword, I immediately agreed. Alas, a bit of "Foreword by Chance".

This is a fun book, but it is also a very serious book, one might even call it a survival handbook.

It is a survival handbook for the manager by chance, default or intention. It helps (us) understand ourselves. Helps us understand that we are not alone in being who and what we are. None of us are the perfect manager, none of us are Managers by Divine Design, and that is ok.

It is a survival handbook because it helps us understand our colleagues, it gives us a language and map for navigating the tricky and on occasions treacherous organizational terrain.

Finally, it is a survival book for freshly graduated students. These poor 20'somethings often enter work life totally unprepared for the wonderful but also confusing organizational landscape, and the many species of managers.

My oldest will in a relatively near future leave Copenhagen Business School, I will make certain he has a copy of Angela's book in his hand.

Enjoy,

Per Kristiansen

Warnings

Manager by Chance may seriously harm your health

In *Manager by Chance* any reference to facts or people is purely coincidental. It could not be otherwise. Even the title says so.

Manager by Chance is aimed at managers all over the world.

If humor is not your thing, if you do not have a lighthearted approach to your existence, well, in that case don't open this book. We recommend deeper readings such as *One Hundred Years of Solitude*[1] or quoted manuals of business literature[2]. You have all our respect.

Manager by Chance also speaks to young managers. Life in the company is an incredible experience, a microcosm in the macrocosm of your existence, populated by human beings, archetypes, tics, neuralgia, laughter, sweats, drives, projects, affections, and a few too many hours of work. Hopefully, this reading will make your journey lighter and more enjoyable.

Maybe you too are a manager by chance and don't know it.

---

1 *One Hundred Years of Solitude* (*Cien años de soledad*) is a 1967 novel by Colombian Nobel laureate Gabriel García Márquez.
2 I recommend, if you haven't already read them, classics such as Michael E. Porter's *Competitive Strategy*, 1980, or the timeless *Principles of Marketing* by the father of modern marketing Philip Kotler. Or *Blue Ocean Strategy*, still very valid, by W. Chan Kim and Renée Mauborgne. Let me know what you think or maybe write and recommend your reference books. We will become friends.

Introduction

It is an indisputable truth that no one is born a manager.

Not even the daddy's boys. Not even the grandchildren of great entrepreneurs and tycoons. Not even their neighbors by mileage-epidemiological effect or deskmates by intellectual osmosis. "Hand me the notebook and touch my finger, I become a manager".

It doesn't work that way. There is no such thing as the contact manager, there is no such thing as the passing manager, there is no such thing as the generational manager.

You don't find yourself already in your thirties with suspenders, a 24-hour briefcase and stilettos rhythmically announcing your presence in the company because you are a woman and you have to make yourself respected in an area where machismo is cut with a chainsaw.

No. Managers are also born with their asses in the wind, stomach cramps and tears on their faces. Maybe a few more tears than others because a quarter of the cells in their body already know that one day they will belong to a manager's body.

No one is born a manager. After cutting the umbilical cord, several maternal pacifiers and several handfuls of baby food and purees, they grow up with shiny eyes that observe on the world. Like everyone else. They fall, get up, fall back, fall in love, make mistakes, laugh, cry.

And you don't know how, you don't know why, you don't know when, but at some point you find them behind a desk doing Excel, checking budgets, and entering keywords on

Google Adwords[3], fighting with others over who has it bigger (the number).

There is no such thing as the contact manager, there is no such thing as the transitional manager, there is no such thing as the generational manager.
    Instead, there is the manager and the manager by chance, the fallback manager, the manager by lack of alternatives.
    This is their story. And also that of some of you.

---

3   Google's advertising system is auction-based via keywords. By trivializing it, brands try to intercept, for a fee, the words that allow their product to rank high in search engine searches, the same words with which users search online. The recent SearchGpt could be a game changer.

Who Is a Manager
And especially who is a manager by chance

It is 2003. I am thirty-one years old. It is one o'clock in the morning. The *abat-jour* points to the keyboard of my PC. It's dark all around. The screen projects a horrid Excel. I am finishing the micro profit and loss account for a project that I will present the next day to the Management Board. I repeat: It is 1 a.m. I am tired, spent, stubborn. Working at 1 a.m. is not an achievement, not a privilege. But it's worth it, I tell myself. I will leave my boss speechless.

It's 2007. I am thirty-five years old. I am communication manager. It's always one o'clock in the morning. The *abat-jour* always points to my pc keyboard, only the *abat-jour* is different and the pc is a new model. Laptop. It's still dark all around. The screen is projecting an evolved PowerPoint presentation of yet another last-minute requested project for which I think it is worth it. I am tired but determined. I will leave my boss speechless, a different guy than the one I thought I was leaving speechless in 2003.

It's 2013. I am forty-one years old. I'm a digital marketing manager. It's still one o'clock in the morning. Yes, it's worth it. Sure. The *abat-jour* is gone. There is LED lighting, central, in the room in an industrial setting house. It is no longer dark all around. The screen projects yet another PowerPoint, with tabular elements in it, Excel copy-paste and many, many KPI[4]. Tired? I am, but I'm not giving up. Tomorrow I will leave

---

4   Key performance indicators allow you to measure the progress of a project or business process. There is no manager by chance who doesn't have a large set of KPI's in his portfolio to show off in meetings, boardrooms, Excel, PowerPoint and steering committees.

yet another boss speechless over yet another project that emerged for the umpteenth time at the last moment.

It's 2024. I am fifty-one years old, almost fifty-two. I am marketing and communications manager. It is one o'clock in the morning. There is no *abat-jour*, no LED, no lighting in the room. Yet again it is dark all around and everywhere. I am lying in bed, sleepless. I don't count the sheep. I count how many days, weeks, months, years I have spent working until one in the morning. How many projects requested last minute, how many PowerPoints, how many Excel. How many bosses I thought I was leaving speechless. How many times I thought it was worth it and leaned over the PC automatically. How many friends found themselves compacting PowerPoint and formulating Excel at one in the morning. For all of them for so many times it was worth it.

It is 2024. I am fifty-one years old, almost fifty-two. It is 1:15 in the morning.

I'm a manager. I've always got something to manage. I've always got other people to manage. And projects. And "things". I don't remember clearly how it started. I came to managing in a random, uncalculated, unintentional way. And I know I am not alone. I know that behind those desktops pulsed arrhythmic and sincere hearts of managers by chance, a bold, outraged and proud people.

We have all accepted the challenge, with the lightness of those who feel they have time to decide what to do when they grow up, without realizing that they already are. There it is, on the horizon, the company. There is our desk waiting for us. There is our place marker: ma-na-ger.

THE MANAGER POPULATION

The Climbing Manager

I am what I do.
Reinhold Messner

Imagine a huge mountain, not like Everest, not like K2, but like Thomas Mann's *The Magic Mountain*[5], a shelter and lodging for people who refuse to return to the plains and to their mundane existence. A mythical place near the Hyperuranium[6], a non-place, out of time, from which you can touch Olympus with one finger. A mountain, enchanted indeed, where anything is possible.

Now imagine yourself a guest, albeit momentary, of this sanatorium mountain. In all likelihood you have come to visit an aunt, just as Hans Castorp, a young engineer from Hamburg, in Mann's pages had gone to the Swiss sanatorium in Davos to visit his cousin who was ill with tuberculosis.

That was the summer of 1907. Now we are in the 21st century. You are with your aunt on the main veranda, overlooking the entire valley. You lean out from the little terrace and look down at the bottom of the valley. Do you see that little dot? That tiny dot struggling upward?

It is the climbing manager, in the midst of social climbing.

For the climbing manager, the Management Board is as close as he can get to the enchanted mountain. It is his Davos, it is his magical place. It is the place to which he wants, feels he must belong, as in Aristotle's theory of natural places[7].

---

5   *Der Zauberberg* is a novel by German writer Thomas Mann from 1924.
6   Hyperuranium is an area beyond the heavens, a world in which ideas dwell, described by the Greek philosopher Plato in the *Phaedrus*.
7   In one of the eight books devoted to *Physics*, dated around the fourth century B.C., the Greek philosopher Aristotle explains the theory of natural places: if you move one of the four elements from its natural place, it tends to return to it. As a stone thrown into the sea returns to the earth, as

For Aristotle, the natural motion of earth and water is downward, that of air, fire and the climbing manager is upward.

The climbing manager is an expert in the organizational ladder. At home he has all the equipment: flattery, chatter, smiles, personal favors are better for him than climbing boots for icefall and mixed climbing.

If you want to travel, he organizes your trip. If you love music, he brings you an original Miles Davis recording from 1952. If you like soccer, he gets you grandstand tickets. If you appreciate good food, he cooks for you. If you want to taste wine, he brings you the finest Chardonnay from his cellar. If you want to read but are tired, he gets you the podcast you've been looking for. The climbing manager is the perfect man at the perfect time.

A sharp observer, goal-oriented mind, summit achievement, he knows exactly what you want when you want it. He has the plush stride, the athletic sprint and sharp reflexes.

A great corporate climber by profession, as soon as he enters a corporate structure he studies it with big smiles, smells it, feels it, chatters, jigs, humors, nods until he figures out who to bet on, which piece is most appropriate to gain the favor of management in the shortest possible time.

Having identified the schemers, she applies herself with the greatest dedication and in total absence of modesty. The consternation of other colleagues does not touch him in the least. A great chamberlain of relations, he silences his neighbor with a few cheap favors, directly proportional to the value the colleague represents in his climb. Management notices, but plays along. It's always handy to have someone to move your car if it's hailing outside. What should not be overlooked, however, is the climber's good faith. Far from being easily labeled as a common careerist, the climbing

---

a bubble of air in water rises to reach the sphere of air where it belongs. Like a manager by chance it returns to the company every day.

manager truly believes that his place is there, high up among the Olympian gods.

Doesn't that tug at your heart? He monopolizes you in the coffee room for dozens of minutes, complaining that he is not properly considered, that he does not have the right framing for his stature, that he is not on the Management Board, but he also reminds you of how much the president enjoyed the last Dom Perignon he got for him or how the manager chooses him as a confidant in the company.

Meanwhile, the climber continues to bestow gifts with the naive, innocent manner of a child who has been yearning since first grade for a Van Basten[8] figurine and in return, now that he is in fourth grade, offers you his raspberry-caramel lollipop. Eventually, lollipop after lollipop, Chardonnay after Chardonnay, you too will give in, addicted to the sugar, totally won over by the enveloping flavor of the caramel.

In the end, the climber truly deserved that figurine. That lounger on the terrace of the enchanted mountain is now his.

---

8   Marco Van Basten, a great Dutch soccer striker. He played for Milan, an Italian soccer team, for many years. He is considered one of the best players in the history of soccer.

The Highlander Manager

> *The length of a film should be directly related to the endurance of the human bladder.*
>
> Alfred Hitchcock[9]

I don't know any manager who gets sick. Better, we get sick, yes, we're human, but we don't allow room for sickness, strained as we are by habit to production. Indefensible, continuous, no escape.

You find us in hospital waiting rooms with laptops in hand, sprawled over our phones as we type yet another email with our index finger at lightning speed. As everyone coughs, and so do we, we promptly answer the call to duty with our cool new Bluetooth headsets, contemptuous of disinfectants and bacilli.

We live, we managers by chance, by an eternal paradox: we subject our bodies, novice Atlases, to impervious pressures, subjugated by the continuous drive to perform, and when the body reminds us of its existence with a big, resounding, shattering sneeze, we shut it up with the first analgesic pill in hand, only to return to complain about this affectless, joyless life caused by our own "circus-like" behavior.

But, as in all self-respecting circumstances, the sick manager, heedless of the transience of his body, has his own oppositional doppelgänger in the Highlander manager.

The Highlander manager excels, always, even when he peels a banana in less than two seconds, putting the residue back into the organic compost at the mechanical pace of a highly skilled worker, as if it were an Olympic discipline. He

---

9   Of all the films by the master of the thriller, the one that comes closest to the corporate world is *International Intrigue*, the 1959 feature film starring a publicity agent, played by the charming Cary Grant.

gets up at five in the morning to jog *en plein air*, heedless of the frost, heedless of the cold, heedless of the aerosol-effect mugginess that not even an asthmatic, trained in breathlessness, can cope with.

Heedless and that's all.

The Highlander manager is metaperformant, a performance of performance. Super-trained and super-attentive to his nutrition, knows chemistry and nature inside out, knows how to supplement, best friends with the pharmaceutical companies of dietary supplement production.

Because, let's face it, in a world in which the permutation of form for substance reigns indefatigably and all our lives revolve around the concept of performance, the manager, whether by chance or not, feels he needs a little help to become what the context asks him to become: the performance manager.

That is why he relies on brand-name sportswear. Because there is no trained manager who is not designer. The bootie, the tracksuit, the sweatshirt, the gadget, the smartwatch with built-in heart rate counter, step counter, wrinkle counter, white hair counter, everything counter.

A yoga enthusiast, meditation devotee, sugar enemy, and quinoa religionist, he has one unsurpassed Achilles' heel: hypochondria. If you want to get rid of it, you know how. One sneeze in the middle of a meeting, even a simulated one, and that's it: the Highlander manager leaves the field, even without saying goodbye. He keeps his distance, forerunner of Covid prophylaxis, with sanitizing wipes always at hand.

The Highlander Manager took this health thing more seriously than others, plumping up his hygiene kit with additional devices and accessories: the saturimeter, the swab set, the serums, the Ffp2 masks, the Ffp2 mask cover, washable and complete with embroidered initials HM (Highlander Manager), the sanitized mask holder, the hand sanitizer, the face sanitizer, the eyebrow sanitizer, the anti-acne mask, the home disinfectant spray, the car disinfectant spray, the subscription to clinical journals, the epidemiological news, the chat with the health minister's neighbor who, because of proximity, gets vital news first.

In the pandemic period, the Highlander manager became champion of the living room spot run and terrace marathon. He implemented his yogic techniques to reinforce positive thinking, a true boon to the immune system.

But if you sneeze during a meeting, even if you're on Teams, even if you're on Zoom, even if you're on Google Meet, he'll disconnect your connection. Forever, unless you show a clean bill of health.

The Cassandra Manager

> *The best way to predict the future is to create it.*
> Peter Drucker[10]

If you are a manager in the 2020s, you most likely belong to Generation X or are a Millennial[11].

It goes very badly for you if you are a Baby Boomer manager. In that case the generational leap with the exponential age we are living in is a real quantum gap. Like the ones in Star Trek[12]. But if you're Baby Boomer, let's face it, you don't read a manager's manual by chance. You don't care about getting out of it. You just wait for retirement.

For everyone else there's continuing education. The desperate informational chase against time to be able to converse with current events and the Zs, the digital natives, the overlords of our time. Wean, attentive, technological, bread-and-digital eaters. But also very selective, specialized, without that flying patent that makes us of other generations lift off the ground by helicopter to contextualize the situation, encompass the case, look at the horizon and glimpse the new.

If you are dealing with digital natives, you know that they are not going to make it on their own, not yet, but you also know that you, today, cannot make it without them.

---

10   Austrian economist known for his management theories. Famous for his publications in such quoted journals as "The Economist", "The Wall Street Journal", and "Harvard Business Review". We attribute the goal-setting theory to him.

11   Do you want to know which generation you belong to? The Baby Boomers generation includes those born between 1946 and 1964, Generation X between 1965 and 1980, the Millennials or Generation Y between 1980 and 2000, and the digital natives, the Zeticians were born after 2000.

12   Warp drive is a type of propulsion that causes the spacecraft in the glorious Star Trek television series to sail at speeds faster than light, to make a real leap in time and space.

That's the fairy tale you tell yourself every night. Until one day, in between calls, you catch a glimpse of that rampant flicker in the gaze of the nearest Z, the one you greeted, the one you accompanied to the boss's office, to the kitchen pantry and in search of toilet paper, him, the very one, and you vividly picture him as he pulls your chair aside and drapes his shawl over your shoulders taking possession of your mouse.

It is also possible that you are an aging digital person. One who caught digital early, as if it were a disease, and developed antibodies to it, saving yourself from it. Or so you think. Because in reality, if you are a digital old-timer, it is as if you live in the middle-earth, neither Elf nor Orc, neither Gandalf nor Sauron[13], neither Z nor Boomer. You are not native like the Zs and you are not avulsed like the Boomers. You don't speak technicalese and you don't appeal to memories of using a typewriter like inky-flavored madeleines[14]. You get by, you know how to run a SEM campaign[15], you recognize a digital ecosystem when you see it, you can manage website developments.

And that's where you're wrong. Because if you do know how to do it, you're surrounded on the one hand by young Zeticians who flaunt tecnichese at you like it's an HTML language you don't know, and on the other hand by managers like you who aren't digital old-timers, they're just old-timers, terrified to death of what they don't know, passive aggressive in lineage.

---

13 Sworn enemies, Gandalf the White and the Dark Sauron are two characters from *The Lord of the Rings* the wonderful trilogy by John Ronald Reuel Tolkien.
14 In one of the most famous passages in Marcel Proust's *On Swann's Side*, a madeleine pastry dipped in tea brings back to the protagonist the feeling of joy experienced years earlier, in Cambray, with the madeleines offered by Aunt Leonia, soaked in lime tea. The past becomes the present.
15 SEM stands for search engine marketing, one of the branches of web marketing consisting of SEO, search engine optimization, and SEA, search engine advertising. The goal of SEM techniques is to convert as many target audience as possible to the website and induce them to take various actions, from reading a magazine to registering for a newsletter to buying online on e-commerce platforms.

And if you keep the former at bay because they are younger, armed with looks of condescension that they throw your way from time to time, along the lines of "he's my boss, but he doesn't understand a thing about reservation"[16], the others, the older ones, are a tough nut to crack.

You try to explain digital to them as if it were a Gordon Ramsey recipe, you go out of your way to repeat how campaigns work, you remind them that Google doesn't favor your promo over those of competitors because you write "Eighty euros off" in the advert, you explain to the point of dysphonia that there are no clean leads[17] or dirty leads by desperately clinging to the most common tautology in the company: "a lead is a lead". You do this, always, repeatedly, every day, several times a day. And one of those days, with no particular surprises, you realize that you are a Cassandra[18]. You didn't mean to be, but you are.

The Cassandra manager knows, is a repository of information that has real value and public utility. A bearer of good, Cassandra would like to share it with others. Open it to the world like a Pandora's box full of colorful, fragrant, fresh flowers. But facing Cassandra, a gnoseological relativist by choice, is the absolute truth of rejection. Rejection out of fear of being unhinged, rejection of the unknown, the horribleness of emptiness.

Cassandra repeats her digital positioning nursery rhymes every day, but no one believes her. Keywords, adwords, CPA, CPL, CPM[19]. They prefer not to see, they prefer not to know.

---

16 Purchasing online advertising space at cpm (cost per miles impressions) and otherwise with a guaranteed budget. This is a traditional advertising model used in brand awareness campaigns.

17 A lead is a business contact. A lead is generated when the company obtains references and personal information to contact a user again and make a purchase proposal.

18 A figure in Greek mythology, daughter of Hecuba and Priam, king of Troy, she was a priestess of the Temple of Apollo and an unheard prescient. She predicted the fall of Troy, but no one believed her. In the company we know something about this.

19 Let's dive into the digital marketing world. Keywords are the keywords

25

They prefer to leave Cassandra to her fate, to a sad story, mocked as she is for her visions, denuded of the prospects of listening and solution.

There he is in the coffee room, with his loneliness and frustration. He knows in his foresight that when the prophecy comes true the aged will take possession of it by functional phagocytosis, as if they were the first to have formulated it, the first to glimpse it live.

Cassandra is neither Elf nor Orc, neither Gandalf nor Sauron, neither Z nor Boomer. Cassandra is digital elderly.

---

entered by users into search engines. The SEO and SEA businesses try with SEO copywriting and advertising work to include those words in their content by intercepting searches and gaining views. CPA, cost per action; CPL, cost per lead; CPM, cost per miles impression, are economic metrics for evaluating online advertising actions.

The Pontius Pilate Manager

> *Washing hands can keep you healthy and prevent the spread of respiratory and diarrheal infections.*
>
> Centers for Disease Control and Prevention

He is always smiling, peaceful and sly. He pats you on the back, always says yes, gives you a seat, stops by to say hello, offers you coffee, opens the door for you, collects your packages, nods as you nod, shakes his head as you shake it, and as soon as he can, he delegates his tasks to you.

It is the seductive technique of the Pontius Pilate manager. Yes, that's the one. The superficial, seductive one, the one who savors it all[20], every word, every desk, every compass, every stapler and every door handle he can get his hands on.

The Pontius Pilate manager, the tiger we all know. It doesn't matter what gender he has, male, female, transgender. It doesn't matter his sexual choices, his height, his hair color, his exact weight. And your doesn't matter either. Because when he is around, you are the prey. Whether you want it or not.

The tiger knows exactly what he wants from you and knows only one way to get it: seduction.

It's true. Some tiger managers practice seduction for seduction's sake, from a narcissistic perspective of pure sensory gratification. They don't care what you have to give them. They care about having you. Even if only for a moment, because the next moment already belongs to someone else.

But solipsistic tigers, let's face it, are rare. They almost always have an ulterior motive, an objective, a goal: that, first and foremost, of personal peace of mind, of their own bene-

---

20 "Fate l'amore con il sapore" lit. translated 'makes love with flavor' is a play on the Muller yogurt slogan. "Love every bit" is the Muller yogurt international slogan.

fit. They don't want trouble, they don't want problems. If they can shine they shine, but when the going gets tough they eclipse themselves in the shadows, leaving the discomfort to someone else, in a colossal metaphorical coarse washing of hands. We can hear the splash of icy water from here. Better known as "manager appearances" because of the rapidity of their spills, you find them participating in meetings that with their input become mammoth soap operas, not dilated places where the tiger disrupts the order of ideas, intervenes prolixly explaining and explaining himself, asking and wondering about things completely clear to most, going over previous episodes, dismembering them like a Russian deconstructionist and reassembling them Picasso-style, to the general dismay of those present, driven to exasperation and intestinal prolapse. And at the finest moment, when he has totally derailed the meeting with a dispersiveness that has not even the hint of professionalism, he leaves for another engagement. When it comes to taking responsibility, the tiger manager is not there. He is elsewhere. Yet this obnoxious and counterproductive behavior generates in most annoyance but not anger, not furious anger. Because the Pontius Pilate manager continues to smile, to offer you coffee, to open the door for you, to nod when you nod, to shake his head as you shake it, appealing to the Fifth Amendment of your mirror neurons[21].

You look at him with a mixture of compassion and annoyance, like a poor fellow who is basically not living up to himself, a victim of his own insubstantiality, but you are instead oblivious to his seductive technique and to having fallen into his sphere of action.

Suddenly you nod when he nods, shake your head when he shakes it. And you want to do the work.

---

[21] The discovery of mirror neurons is attributed to the research group of the Department of Neuroscience at the University of Parma, led by Professor Giacomo Rizzolatti. They are particular neurons that are activated on imitation of the other.

The Manager in Love

Love is in the air, everywhere I look around
Love is in the air, every sight and every sound
And I don't know if I'm being foolish
Don't know if I'm being wise
But it's something that I must believe in
And it's there when I look in your eyes.
                                    John Paul Young[22]

There is manager in love and manager in love.

The manager who has taken a lurch and is swaying "ebetically" through the halls with scattered and unfocused demeanor (ah, *l'amour*) tends to be a fledgling manager, still not devoted to camouflaging the feeling, and a young manager, although when love knocks on your door there is no dignity to spare. Isn't it wonderful?

There is also the manager who is in love with his family, the one who, for better or worse, makes you want to have one, with a picture of his children on his desk and a ready answer on his cell phone if his or her life partner calls.

The last category, the one we will dwell on, is the dangerous liason, the affair, the corporate affair.

It is unavoidable. Raise your hand if any of us managers have not had, in our past or present, an affair with a colleague, with an office neighbor, with a professional partner, with a consultant, with a client, with a person we met in the workplace. Managers by chance spend a dozen hours a day sprawled over the exact same desk, come out, perhaps, on Friday night projected on a hopeful weekend that often results in unconditional respite from office drudgery, household chores, and necessary expenses. On Monday it all be-

---

[22] These are the first stanzas of the very famous song *Love Is in The Air* released in 1977 by Australian singer John Paul Young.

gins again, in a Vichian circle of historical ebb and flow where the hamster in the wheel is ultimately you.

It goes without saying, then, that statistically the opportunities for meeting and relationship possibilities are concentrated to a greater extent in three specific cases: dating chats, where you expose yourself to a bulimic jungle of satiating appetites, of whatever kind they may be, sexual, affective, verbal; for the more reluctant and old fashioned, supermarkets - doesn't Maslow[23] speak of basic needs? - and work environments.

If the manager falls in love at work, well, it goes without saying, he has to be very, very careful. It is red alert to the nth degree.

No one tells you this, but it is the truth, even for those who, like me, are gnoseological relativists and do not believe in the absolute. It is unquestionable truth that horizontal relationships are allowed at work but verticality should be strongly avoided. I say this for your sake. No allusions to twisted Kamasutra positions. If you fall in love with your colleague in another function, that's fine. If you're from purchasing and you date someone in sales, it's okay. If you're from product marketing and you break up with someone from IT, that's fine. But if you're an intern and you get the boss lady or if you're a function manager and you flirt with your subordinate or your junior, there you're trouble. You can do it, but rest assured that someone is going to get hurt.

Gender difference does matter to some extent in these circumstances. It is a sadly widely held view that if you are female you want to get ahead, if you are the male boss you are the cool type picks up younger employees.

In fact, whichever way you spin it, the result is bad.

A young person, whatever gender he or she belongs to,

---

[23] Abraham Maslow was an American psychologist, known for his pyramid, the theory on the hierarchy of needs, from physiological needs at the base to the needs for self-actualization and self-acceptance at the top, via the needs for security, belonging and esteem.

who becomes infatuated with power, represented by the person to whom he or she answers professionally, will always see his or her professional abilities questioned. An "expert" who has with one of his subordinates will always have his professional seriousness questioned, as if from then on any decision he makes is guided by his sexual instincts.

Retrograde? Retrograde. But life is unfair, and you might as well know from the start what, if anything, to dodge.

So what about Tom Cruise and Renée Zellweger in *Jerry Maguire*[24]? James Spader and Maggie Gyllenhaal in *Secretary*[25]? Spencer Tracy and Katherine Hepburn in *The Almost Private Secretary*[26]?

It worked out well for them. True, there is one exception: that of great love, that of sincere feeling, which overcomes great obstacles, strong in its substantial depth. But even in this case, it pains me to tell you, you rarely have a chance.

If you fall in love with your boss or your subordinate and decide that the feelings you are feeling is worth it, there is in fact only one thing you can do: one of you must change companies. And if math is not an opinion, the one who has to clear his or her desk is usually the one who holds the least important position in the corporate organizational chart.

If, on the other hand, it is not love, but a dangerous liason, be very very good at keeping it quiet, at not giving rise to the chatter and misunderstandings that, even if you think you couldn't give a damn today, will ruin your career tomorrow, in an environment where reputation is paramount, in an

---

[24] *Jerry Maguire*, a 1996 film directed by Cameron Crowe, is a corporate must-see. There is no manager who is unfamiliar with the scene in which Jerry, played by Tom Cruise, while talking with his one-time client, Cuba Gooding Jr. by energetically repeating the phrase, "Show me the money". "Help me help you" is another gem in the film, often used by managers frustrated with their managers.

[25] Directed by Steven Shainberg in 2002, the film is about love as a meeting of two compatible pathologies, even and especially in the office.

[26] Walter Lang's 1957 masterpiece, the film stars Spencer Tracy and Katherine Hepburn as the real-life protagonists of a secret love affair between colleagues that lasted twenty-six years.

age when form is substance and words you give no weight to are ultimately a boulder.

So don't get caught in the closet, don't send dating proposals using your company email or cell phone, don't go out with him or her to clubs where you can easily get caught. Do what you want to do discreetly.

Remember that you could always end up like Michael Douglas and Demi Moore in the Michael Crichton movie *Revelations*[27]: not well. And after all, the story between Bridget Jones[28] and Hugh Grant did not capitulate into marriage either.

I mean, young hopeful girl or vigorous son at the gates of the world: if you fall in love with your boss or you just want to do them, I understand. I vaguely recall that hormonal upheaval that power can give.

You, however, should take your aunt's advice: make yourself a sacher torte and leave it alone.

---

[27] 1994 film directed by Barry Levinson and based on Michael Crichton's novel of the same name.
[28] *Bridget Jones's Diary* is a 2001 film directed by Sharon Maguire and based on the novel of the same name by Helen Fielding.

The Incontinent Manager

> *To eliminate the concept of waste means to design things-products, packaging, and systems-from the very beginning on the understanding that waste does not exist.*
> William McDonough[29]

Each of us has encountered along the corporate corridors at least once in our lives the incontinent manager, the emotional incontinent one, the one who lights up like a spark to prove to himself that he has a feeling and to the rest of the world that he exists, the one who doesn't listen to what you say and out of sheer egoic-defensive necessity attacks you, in the absence of data.

To defend his fragile and insecure little self from attacks that are not there, except in his frustrated and imbecilic imagination.

It is difficult to deal with the incontinent manager. He is the one who reasons from the gut, he is energetic, he is the one who, when confronted with your thoughtful and judicious work, uses expressions like "throwing his heart over the fence", heedless of the untenability of what he is saying and the risk the company is facing.

The incontinent manager wastes a lot of your time. And your patience.

But the incontinent manager doesn't care. He cares about the reassuring cuddle of the immediate response to his need to exist.

Often, when emotional incontinence arrives so does in-

---

[29] Renowned architect and author whose outreach and architectural works underlie a philosophy devoted to environmental and social sustainability and the sustainable recycling of materials.

competence, the momentary obnubilation of *res cogitans*[30], even in the most intelligent managers.

The incontinent manager is not focused on the what, he is focused on the relationship. If the relationship does not satisfy him, he flushes not only the handle but also the most valuable project down the toilet. And he does this by contradicting himself. Quite possibly that project a year ago had also been approved by him. Perhaps he supported it first, for momentary gain. But now he has forgotten about it and revokes it.

No, it is not easy to manage the incontinent manager. You don't manage him head-on, except by making the situation worse. You don't handle him by avoiding him, except by finding yourself in even bigger trouble.

But there is a way. It is a welcoming, inclusive, understanding way. And it is so fashionable. Because great things can come out of compassion.

If you are faced with an incontinent manager, you have to treat him as such. You have to think of him as a person suffering from severe colitic spasms. He squirms, he struggles, he suffers. His belly aches. He is in pain.

Until he breaks free. Until he breaks free with a loud, thunderous, pestilential fart.

My goodness, you will say. For such things there are designated places, universally called bathrooms. There are muscles to contract to manage the sphincter. The exercise of restraint is what marks the transition from youth to maturity, you remind me.

True, undoubtedly.

Nevertheless, if you are faced with a pathological fart, there are a few moves you can make to save your queen[31].

---

30 It was the French philosopher René Descartes who first made, in the early decades of the seventeenth century, the distinction between res cogitans - thought - and res extensa - matter - decreeing the rationalistic approach of the Western world for many centuries until the arrival of quantum physics.

31 In the game of chess, the queen is considered the most powerful piece because of her ability to move nonchalantly across the board. The game

Confronting him by accusing him and urging him never to do it again is a risky move. I can already see rooks and knights falling. "You are a fart! You are a fart! What a stench! What a stink!" I used to say in the early days, in my first experiences with emotional incontinents. The reactions were the worst. When cornered, the manager would get excited and fart even more, choking you completely with his exhalations.

No, candor with the emotional incontinent is not a pursuable path. Conversely, it is not right for you to suffer the stench of others. It is not right for you to be the victim of smelly, corrosive odors.

There is therefore only one thing to do.

Open the windows wide to ventilate the room and, if the stench persists, leave the room.

Better times will come, believe me. The farts will subside and everyone can start breathing again.

If the incontinent manager detonates in loud, corrosive performances, leave, take away his audience.

Left alone with his stench, he will subside. Or he will choke to the point of fainting.

---

of chess also has its usefulness applied to business reality and can teach strategy makers how to move, looking forward and thinking backward, as the great visionaries, Steve Jobs, Bill Gates, Jeff Bezos and Elon Musk, do.

The Penelope Manager

> *I used to play with great seriousness. At one point my games were called art.*
>
> Maria Lai[32]

Beware of Manager Penelope if you care about your nerves and the survival of the species.

Manager Penelope seduces all us Proci managers by day by weaving thread after thread, stitch after stitch, admirable canvases, only to secretly unravel them in the evening and start over again the next morning with her, dreamy gaze, eyelashes poured out on the horizon, hair loose on the peplos. Exactly like Ulysses' wife. But if the literary Penelope knowingly implemented a survival tactic while waiting for her husband's return, our Penelope, the corporate one, waits for no one. She is herself a victim of her own web.

His doing and undoing is not the result of careful reasoning, clever thinking, techniques inferred from Sun Tzu's *Art of War*[33], and is not aimed at achieving a phantom goal. Rather, it is the outcome of a confused and insecure mind, the birth of not knowing how to do, the translation into action of non-choice in power.

At first you don't notice it. At first glance, manager Penelope seems to be on the ball, vertically prepared and intransigent toward any meddling. Annoyed by those who resist him, he manifests from the start that he knows his stuff,

---

32 A Sardinian artist and weaver, Maria Lai is remembered as a child artist, for the games of weaving, writing and rewriting that appear in her works. Sometimes with the manager Penelope there is a suspicion that in her unraveling there is a strong component of childlike play.

33 A treatise on military strategy attributed to the general and philosopher Sun Tzu, who presumably lived between the 6th and 5th centuries BC. No manager should cross the corporate threshold without reading it.

taking positions that are often as rigid as a Greek statue in order not to yield a step, all in all heedless of the motives of others.

Trying to soften Penelope is a challenge you can lose, not for lack of tenacity, but for lack of listening. Penelope goes on like a train on its track, unheeded at railroad crossings, in autism-afflicted caterpillar mode.

Set it in front of a decision, however, and its weaving, intertwined nature leaks out with an instantaneousness that not even the Road Runner appeared as quickly before Wile E. Coyote on the precipice of the Grand Canyon.

Prepared on the surface but not so much in delving into the matter, incapable of taking responsibility, fearful even of his own shadow, manager Penelope surrounds himself with a bevy of advisers who could intimidate the court of Sun King. At the mercy of now one, now the other, depending on the moment and the matter, he does not move a finger without their consent, deferring answers to the next installment.

Watching him closely, once you peel back the veil of Maya[34], you understand that that initial rigidity was not overconfidence but fear, that that brisk pace was not devoted to the achievement of the goal but to the fear of being arrested and not knowing how to respond.

Barefaced, the real job of the manager Penelope roughly approaches the realm of public relations. Penelope slavishly reports what is communicated to him by consultants, suppliers, partners, and other colleagues at work tables, exponentially stretching the project's time frame in a collective ping pong that leads to exhaustion.

Penelope does not unravel her web, but destroys yours, contradicting in the next installment what was stated in the

---

34 In *The World as Will and Representation* of 1819 Philosopher Arthur Schopenhauer expounds his theory of life as an innate dream and adopts the concept of Maya's veil from Hindu culture. Like the veil of Isis, the veil of Maya comes between the individual's consciousness and perception of reality and reality itself.

previous one, in an informational short-circuit and a continual retracing of her steps.

A great organizer of meetings, where he gathers dozens and dozens of professionals around a table for hours on end, he immobilizes the entire company on decisions that should simply be made without hesitation or continuous revisiting of what has been previously defined.

A meeting with Penelope is scientific proof of the existence of historical Vichian cycles and recycles[35], the pejorative variant of Lavoisier's physical law of "nothing is created, nothing is destroyed", but here nothing is transformed, a mega-screen projection complete with popcorn of the 1990s film *Groundhog Day*. You look circumspectly around and feel like Bill Murray, trapped in a time loop, stuck in *Groundhog Day*[36].

With manager Penelope you don't get out, you'll never get out, unless you oust him, unless you give in to his pathological insecurity and make the decision for him. Only then, only when, with your nerves on edge and the temptation to catch a life sentence for first-degree manslaughter, you have exposed yourself in a matter not your own, then Penelope will beat a retreat, delegating all responsibility, error and misfortune to you.

While dwelling in the same semantic field of non-choice, Penelope differs from her brother Pontius Pilate in timing and methods.

Manager Pilate is not interested in taking a path and manifests this to you from the very beginning, with no risk of deferment in the time frame. He takes it light-heartedly, with that everlasting sly smile of his.

---

[35] At the turn of the late 17th and early 18th centuries, the Neapolitan philosopher Giambattista Vico formulated the theory of the cyclical nature of history by inserting the concept of historical ebbs and flows that evolve humanity from fantasy to reason.

[36] A 1993 comedy directed by Harold Ramis, *Groundhog day* recounts the exploits of meteorologist Phil Connors, played by Bill Murray, who wakes up every day on February 2, Groundhog Day, a U.S. and Canadian holiday.

Penelope, on the other hand, would like to make that choice, but she is unable to and is not even aware of it. She is lost in her mind like *The Twelve Tasks of Asterix*[37], like Ariadne in the labyrinth of the Minotaur[38], like my uncle behind the wheel with an Eskimo's sense of direction in the desert.

---

37   *Les douze travaux d'Astérix* is a 1976 animated film based on the Asterix comic book series by Goscinny and Uder.
38   In Greek mythology Ariadne, princess of Crete, fell in love with Theseus and equipped the latter with a ball of wool to enable him to kill the Minotaur, inhabitant of the labyrinth, and return home. The Athenian hero would abandon her on the island of Naxos.

The Aging Manager

> *To be consumed preferably by...*
>
> A milk carton

Tick tock. Tick tock. Tick tock.

It's not the biological clock. It's the corporate clock. The one that for years has stretched your time by nailing you to your desk around the clock as if it were always morning. Now that you are in your fifties it informs you, "That's all, thank you. You can go". Unaware of the fact he gave you most of the wrinkles and carpal tunnel over the years. Heedless of your abilities. Of your vivid eyes and experienced mind. Like with an old shoe.

We don't say this out of politeness, but that's how it is. At fifty a man reaches his professional maturity, he is cool, he is powerful, he is sexy. A woman is at her expiration date.

No background feminism, no reverse discrimination. Just a healthy, life-giving dialogue with reality.

Reaching fifty, a woman struggles to retrain, to obtain positions of greater prestige, to see the credibility recognized that only a year before was her hallmark.

The most naive do not believe it. The most successful ones deny it. But I do. I know that when you turn forty-nine, you are one year away from being well served. I know that this is the time to choose how to age.

I know it and I knew it before, of course. I knew it not by intuition, but by reading. Reading the faces of female colleagues over fifty who, no matter how well prepared, have seen themselves shelved in the company. Overtaken by rampant co-workers who took their positions in the blink of an eye. Overtaken by events. Watched as a young student, full of high hopes, looks at a fossil of the Valdarno[39]. With horror at the passage of time. With the conceit of youth, as if it won't happen to him someday. Like a mammoth. Like a milk carton gone bad. Like Gloria Swanson in *Sunset Boulevard*[40], without the consolation of a William Holden warming your bed.

I knew it, then. For a long time already. That same time that nailed me to my desk twelve hours a day. With projects, meetings, goals, management, misinformation, tantrums, solutions. That same time that it mislead me. And now it's gone. You find yourself over 50 behind the desk like Pirandello's embellished old lady[41], who uses excessive makeup to earn the loyalty and affection of her younger husband.

Some say to themselves, "I will not let them shelve me", and leave first. The runaways.

There are those who adopt the dynamic wallflower position, adjust and stand back to the wall shoehorning, passing photocopies that no longer need to be printed. Like elderly women dressed up at weddings, sitting on the sidelines as they move their little feet and heads rhythmically, no longer having the strength to dance.

Some put themselves in the trenches and won't let go of

---

39 The Upper Valdarno, the valley of the Arno River in Tuscany, a region of Italy, is one of the most important sites of vertebrate fossil finds in the world in terms of origin and morphological conformation. Today many finds are housed by the Museum of Natural History in Florence and metaphorically in some companies.

40 *Sunset Boulevard* is a 1950 film noir directed by Billy Wilder and starring William Holden and Gloria Swanson, a silent film actress on the waning path with the advent of sound.

41 In the 1908 critical essay *L'umorismo* (*On Humor*), Luigi Pirandello uses the figure of the embellished old lady to explain the difference between comic, warning of the opposite, and humor, feeling of the opposite. If you see a lady of a certain age walking by with excessively gaudy make-up you perceive that her behavior is the opposite of what you might expect from a woman of her age. And you laugh. But if you knew that the lady is married to a man much younger than her and that the make-up is her way of not losing her husband, then you may feel some compassion. Humor is the two-faced herma laughing at the crying of the opposite face. Humor is the daily mood of a manager by chance.

the position. One day they will find themselves moved like parcel post to the outskirts of the empire. Sunshine. Standing still in the face of the frantic and inconclusive running of others.

Then there are those on Plan B. Those who give themselves a year to figure out what to do with their existence. Yes, they could have thought about it sooner, but they put it off and put it off, going with the flow of life, doing things, seeing people arrive at forty-nine year old - forty-nine - with a young girl's heart, a burning imagination and a body wracked with ailments to carefree wonder, "What am I going to do when I grow up?"

Tick tock. Tick tock. Tick tock. The hope of an existence-resolving year is a chimera. I know. A way to procrastinate the inevitable meltdown. An alibi for stalling.

"Nothing different is going to happen in a year", says a little voice in the head to those in Plan B. "At least you've still got another year!" mutters another, in a dichotomous dialogue that leads them to think about giving it all up to be a fine bulb florist, cookie baker or embroiderer of fine weaves. I am currently holding the crochet hook.

There is always the last resort, the promise of Prince Charming. The corporate Prince Charming doesn't kiss you. If he does it is sexual harassment, unless you are consenting, and then it is an affair.

Corporate Prince Charming gives you the role of your dreams, assigns you the budget of your dreams, and elevates you to the position you deserve: the throne. Without you having to do anything. Without you having to ask, without you having to remember, without you having to lose your dignity. Just like that, just because you are you. Magnificent as you are. It protects you from all evil, finds you smart even in your fifties, and commands respect from the rest of the corporate rabble. Always.

While waiting for the corporate Prince Charming, I learned

how to work the Y-stitch from a crochet guru on TikTok. I expect to finish the quilt in a year. Because there are many drafts in the suburbs.

The Performance Manager

> *I'm not afraid of death; I just don't want to be there when it happens.*
>
> Woody Allen

In a world in which the supremacy of signifier over signified reigns indefatigably and all our lives revolve around the concept of performance, the manager, whether by chance or not, feels he needs a little help. Especially if you take away his chocolate and chips dispensing machine, an oasis of peace and reassurance, a trusted Linus blanket throughout the 1990s and the first two decades of the 2000s.

Then came the concept of the forever manager, the round-the-clock, healthy, focused manager that all managers on the face of the earth yearn for as a viable palliative to the arrival of the first artificial intelligence manager. When the A.I. manager will exist[42], at last the accidental manager can retire.

"A manager is forever. A manager is for life" read on the label of every manager, next to the words "Resilient leader" and "not afraid of impropriety".

---

[42] Digital transformation and artificial intelligence reshape corporate organizational architecture. Today we talk about predictive decision making, a topic that raises inevitable ethical questions and potential legal implications. It is discussed in the *European Parliament Resolution* of February 16, 2017, which could envision, in the long run, the establishment of a legal status for forms of artificial intelligence capable of autonomous decision making and independent interaction with others. In April 2021, the European Commission presented a plan on AI and launched in January 2024 a package to support startups and SMEs in artificial intelligence. On Oct. 30, 2023, the United States signed executive order (E.O.) on the Safe, Secure and Reliable Development and Use of Artificial Intelligence. One reassurance: under current regulations, at least up to the time this book was published, no algorithm can be named a member of a BOD.

To speak of a performance manager is tautological, is to decide to engage in rhetorical exercise, in full pleonastic regime. A manager is performance in action, far beyond power. Manager and performance are almost synonymous in every business dictionary on the planet. If you do not produce, you are not a manager. If you are not efficient, you are not a manager. If you are not effective, much less so.

We all remember the lecture about the difference between efficiency and effectiveness that our first boss, a management engineer or wannabe, gave us. In a nutshell, effectiveness indicates the ability to achieve the set goal, while efficiency assesses the ability to do so while employing the minimum essential resources. Obviously, the manager embodies both abilities, or at least, in some cases, simulates doing so, but with great dexterity and conviction.

It is precisely when the manager perceives the first signs of failure after years and years of working tirelessly twelve hours a day, years in which weekends mingle with the weekday like a dog chasing its own tail - special signs: continuous polar bear yawns, eyelids closing inexorably on the PC, parked cars found after four neighborhood rounds -, it is when the manager becomes aware that he or she can no longer keep up with the young Gen Z's in the company that help is needed.

That's when the manager enters the wonderful world of nutraceuticals. Supplements to think, supplements to breathe, supplements to empower, supplements-fundamental against cellular aging. Alphalipoics, retinoids, probiotics, coenzyme Q10 like there's no tomorrow, creatine, phosphorus, magnesium and potassium. Plus vitamin D, B vitamins, vitamin C, milk thistle and lactoferrin. Here are the manager's new best friends by accident.

The commissary is legal and active in all pharmacies in the territory. Sometimes you can get them online where the price is advantageous, but for targeted advice the nutraceutical pharmacist is as good as it gets.

Nutraceuticals are our best friends, but we are pharmacists' best friends. And our wallets know something about that. But what more could you want? Even in case it was placebo effect, you feel more vigorous, more alert, smoother, snappier, more energetic, more mnemonic, more responsive than before. Another life.

The dietary supplement is the breakthrough not only for the manager of a certain age. Younger Gen Z's, too, superstimulated by the digital world they belong to, need a little help to facilitate that skill they have least been able to develop during their younger years: concentration. Then mentoring is triggered by the aging manager, preferably an aging digital one to speak the same language, to the younger colleague.

"Junior, you need Power Y. You'll solve any memory or concentration deficit issues", advises Senior. "Thanks, Senior, I'll set up your adwords campaign for you", replies Junior. And suddenly on the ground of integration the two generations meet, each occupying its own place.

The integrator integrates and the performance is saved.

The Dictator Manager

> *For each Joan of Arc there is a Hitler perched at the other end of the teeter-totter.*
> Charles Bukowski

There are those who call him the Sun King, with his bevy of courtiers in tow; there are those who call him the Naked King[43], surrounded by people complimenting his new suit. To him you, the employee, are one of his possessions, you are an object of his spoils, a piece to dispose of at will.

The Great Dictator is the archetype of archetypes in corporate life, the king of all desks.

The Great Dictator does not ask, he demands. He does not say, he demands. He does not want, he waits. And briefly, too. He waits for you to read his mind and for the things he desires to materialize instantly. Just like that, effortlessly.

Tending to be the son of a family-run business, where he was the owner, and tending to be an only child, still stuck in the pubertal phase of "it's mine, it's mine, it's mine" that other human beings experience between eighteen months and three years of age, he could, if he is lucky, become CEO of a multinational corporation, but still remain a Great Dictator and demand, in defiance of the Board of Directors, the exact same things he demanded decades ago when he started running his father's workshop and supervising tank unbolting.

---

[43] *The Emperor's New Clothes* is a fairy tale by Hans Christian Andersen-the father of *The Little Mermaid*-first published in 1837 in *Fairy Tales Told for Children*. A vain monarch is persuaded by two tricksters to wear a wonderful dress that only the unworthy will not be able to see. The subjects, while not seeing it, will sing its praises. "The king is naked" is the exclamation of a child who in the presence of the king will not be able to restrain himself from telling the truth.

No trivialization. The Great Dictator is immediately identifiable; he is perfectly transparent in his dictatorial nature. But there are some precipitous characteristics that will be able to help you manage him, some aspects, common to all Great Dictators, that, if noticed, could save your life in business.

The Great Dictator has a short memory
You believe that you have presented your project to him in great detail and received with difficulty, much much difficulty, his approval in a private appointment you requested months ago with him, having reached the thirteenth version of the same project.

The day after the hard-earned approval you show up freshly shaved in a suit to the Board of Directors to re-submit the idea to the front lines as you and in the presence of him, the boss. It is only then, only when the Great Dictator calls into question every single step of your presentation, every specific dot on the i's, including the decision to make you a banana milkshake that morning for breakfast, it is only then that you realize that you did not meet the Great Dictator the day before.

You met the cousin.

He's the one who attended your speech, he's the one who saw your slides, he's the one who advised you, between the lines, to elide the legal passage, he's the one who told you to have a banana milkshake that morning for breakfast.

It is he, the cousin of the Great Dictator, in every way the same, but not Dictator, just cousin.

Only now do you understand the difference. But you also know that you will never be able to tell them apart. That you will keep running into Cousin and Dictator indifferently and you will never know who approved what. You will only know that the next day one of them, presumably the other, will tell you that the job needs a complete overhaul.

The Great Dictator is a micromanager
A control freak, lacking confidence in his fellow man, as if it had been pulled out of him by the dentist as a child, the Great Dictator is an expert in galactic micromanagement to the nth degree. He scouts out the detail, deconstructs it, manipulates it, an exalted expert in metonymy, the part for the whole, the whole for the part.

Obsessive compulsive, he loses sight of the whole, gets hung up and drags you into a labyrinth of details that not even in Knossos[44] could get out of, defining your value as a person and as a professional on that very single element, a single element that is insignificant to you, so small, so harmless, so for good, insignificant to the project, insignificant to the business organization, insignificant actually even to him, even to the Dictator, but not at that precise moment. Not at that precise moment that gives him the opportunity to prove his superiority over you, his indispensability, his spatial "coolness". He knows, he sees, he does not underestimate.

"I'm very concerned", he tells you greedily on issues that to you and everyone else are emeritus bullshit.

"You are not living up to your role", he asserts sternly, alluding to that dot on the i placed too far to the left of the center of gravity that you and others see as perfectly centered instead. On that dot on the i "depends the user experience of the consumer who because of that microscopic dot on the i, perhaps too small, will no longer buy our product y", he presses. "The reputation of product y will ruin the perception on the whole range x and conversely on the brand and therefore on our company. In two seconds' time, management, seeing the dot on the i, will consider our business

---

[44] Knossos is the most important archaeological site of Magna Graecia, located in the central part of the island of Crete. There stood a legendary labyrinth, which according to Greek mythology was commissioned to Daedalus and his son Icarus by King Minos to enclose the Minotaur, a monstrous creature born from the meeting of the king's wife Pasiphae with a white bull.

plan unsustainable. The BOD will not approve the budget. Our company will go bankrupt. We will all lose our jobs. That dot on the i will bankrupt the company. You will bankrupt the company", he concludes.

And as you lie overwhelmed and mortified, as in your body of manager by chance a now familiar feeling rises from deep within your gut, that mixture of unbearability and humiliation that reaches down your throat, as in your mind the usual "I don't want any more" appears in phosphorescent letters, as all this occurs within you, you intercept the Dictator's satisfied ego in his gaze.

He leaves the room like a cheetah after a feast, satiated, powerful, and light-hearted. He has succeeded in venting his existential frustration on others. He has blown his pestilential breath all over you and now he has no more belly cramps.

He is light, happy, has found his place in the world.

The Great Dictator has a fear of emptiness
Micromanageriality is often associated with a tendency to paroxysmal and indiscriminate accumulation of projects, of KPI, without priority.

Everything is fundamental, everything is decisive depending on the mood, depending on the moment. The Great Dictator imposes, greedily, project after project on his employees. A quintessential bulimic, a victim of horror vacui, he does not know what operativeness means because he has often had the good fortune or the merit of not working his way up the ladder.

That is why he does not recognize the complexity of your work by proclaiming the law of "everything now" throughout the kingdom. That's why he doesn't see you, doesn't recognize your role and, in need of immediate answers, in perpetual anxiety, asks for them from the first person in the hallway, even if unqualified for the answer.

If he decides to intervene, he does so at the drop of a hat.

He sees two details, jumps to conclusions and decides. As usual pissed off. A spurious, sterile pissed off that unfortunately leads to nothing but the dispatch of massive doses of resumes.

The Great Dictator is a fart
I know of no Great Dictator who does not manifest his intestinal nature. The Great Dictator is uncontrolled, tending to be irascible, sometimes fond of profanity.

Seemingly calm, he is suddenly triggered, like a fuse, upon hearing certain words, one is not sure what, and detonates like a pressure cooker with no steam drain diverter.

For the Great Dictator there is no what, only the who. There are no wrong projects, but wrong professionals. Oblivious to what a culture of error is, a lover of personal offense and a devotee of public humiliation, the Great Dictator likes to reprimand bystanders by inviting them to evolution because they always take everything personally.

The Great Dictator may be intelligent, brilliant, instinctive and superintuitive but a troll in emotional intelligence, with all due respect to the trolls of the world.

The Great Dictator is a hypochondriac
The Great Dictator collects specific phobias. Hypochondria is one of them. Tell him you don't feel well, and for a while you will get rid of him. Simulate a hoarseness and that's it.

You find him, oftentimes, engaged in profitable hand washing, in thorough cleansing activities that not even a preoperative surgeon adopts. In the company he has had his own personal bathroom, so as not to share any bacillus with others.

If you work under the Great Dictator, you find your hands corroded by sanitizers, surrounded everywhere by signs reminding you of the compulsory cleanliness before touching any object in the office.

The Great Dictator wants you sanitized and clean, but he doesn't want you at home. The Great Dictator fears loneliness like a gazelle fears the storm, he deflates without an entourage needs the court. He suffers deeply, yearns for audience, presence, listening.

Without others he is lost, tiny in the midst of an empty castle, surrounded by high walls of silence.

The Great Dictator is a showman
The Great Dictator deeply loves drama. If there is no drama he creates it, exaggerating situations and taking them to the extreme, drawing the audience's attention.

Drama that is absorbing existential anxiety, an unbearable anxiety, that the Great Dictator is unsure how to handle. He just wants to get rid of it, as soon as possible, on the first comer with the verbal delicacy that often characterizes him.

Like all actors, the Great Dictator acts. When he needs support he approaches you by denigrating others and recognizing you as the only person who can understand him, the only professional in the field. He obviously does the same with others. Exactly as Nick Nolte's mother did with all her children in Barbra Streisand's wonderful film *The Prince of Tides*[45].

The Great Dictator loves exercise
The Great Dictator is peripatetic. He doesn't talk to you sitting in his office, he talks to you on walks. He loves to be followed by geisha collaborators wherever he wishes. And if you are sitting at your desk immersed in a project, when he bursts into your office you have to drop everything and try to catch every syllable of his whispered speech as he strolls around the room in scattered motion.

Kinetic by constitution, he needs to expiate in movement

---

[45] *The Prince of Tides* is a 1991 film directed by and starring Barbra Streisand, based on Pat Conroy's bestseller of the same name.

his tensions and demands that you do the same. He wants you fit, healthy, always.

You often find him wandering around the offices, listening to production workers, colleagues in the purchasing department from whom he steals indiscretions, front-line issues, opinions. It is on the basis of what they tell him that he makes decisions, in defiance of those who run those departments. Those who are sitting at their desks.

The Great Dictator and women
The Great Dictator is a womanizer, an accumulator of females. A love for women contradicted by his pronounced macho tendencies, alive and well in any board, CDA, meeting and payroll.

I have met Great Dictators with a wife and children at home and a mistress in the company, Great Dictators with affairs with secretaries, Great Dictators with affairs with female workers, Great Dictators with relay passage from one packaging worker to another.

The Great Dictator is a collector of female conquests, tending to be beautiful, tending to be thin, tending to be tall. And he displays them as trophies at the coffee machine or in the parking lot, shameless and proud.

The Great Dictator doesn't do us, he is us
You would like to say that the Great Dictator is a bad person, that he is an asylum lunatic, that he is a first-class asshole, but you really can't. The Great Dictator creates bonds with his victims that only after many years you manage to fully comprehend. Even in the most extreme cases, there remains that memory of a sick person who in the end, in the prevailing pathology, in a crazy way, somehow cared about you. He cared about having you there, to confuse you, to be his nemesis, his goad, his comfort.

You dream of him in your imagination, a new Chaplin,

who, having taken off his uniform, declares to you with puppy-dog eyes as a Brat, stroking his little mustache, "I'm sorry, but I don't want to be an emperor. That's not my business. I don't want to rule or conquer anyone. I should like to help everyone - if possible - Jew, Gentile, black man, white. We all want to help one another. Human beings are like that. We want to live by each other's happiness - not by each other's misery. We don't want to hate and despise one another"[46].

So here is the last requirement: the Great Dictator is an unpunished man. No one knows how, no one knows why, he gets away with it. Always. Even when he is one step away from falling off his horse. Even when someone is about to throw him off the tower.

In the end the Great Dictator remains standing because when you look at him he is just the little dictator of the free state of Bananas[47], with his tics, with his neuroses, he is just a dictator by chance.

Maybe deep down, but really deep down, the Great Dictator is one of us.

---

[46] The excerpt is from Charlie Chaplin's final speech to humanity in the 1940 film *The Great Dictator*. The speech was recently reprised, in April 2020, in the sixty-second commercial *Good morning, humanity* by Lavazza, signed Armando Testa.

[47] *Bananas* is a 1971 film directed by and starring Woody Allen, listed by the American Film Institute as one of the one hundred funniest U.S. films.

The Chanel Manager

> *Vast and innumerable is the extensive generosity of Venu's gifts that multiply, confuse, and intensify the aesthetic impact.*
> James Hillman[48]

When you were a child you were told that clothes make the man, that you should not judge by appearances, that behind a ragamuffin can beat the heart of a rich person, cultured or not, and that inside an Armani can fit an emeritus lout.

Then you grew up, went to college, firmly refractory to permutations of form for substance, and found a job, then another and another.

In each company you learned something: that emotional intelligence matters, that skills are critical but cannot make up for a lack of relationship management skills, that diplomacy wins out in the long run, as does consistency.

You have learned to be disciplined and kindly firm in your positions. You have understood that assertiveness is beautiful but it has a price and you have to be sure whether or not you can pay it. You have learned how to change the toner in your printer, how to reboot a glitching PC, how to recognize an original document from a photocopy. You know what blend of coffee your boss prefers in the morning.

You know that the administration colleague is allergic to pollen and that the sales colleague has been married three times. And you also know that if you are capable, if you are really really capable, there is no mistake that stops you.

---

48 The sentence is from *Aphrodite's Justice* read by the great American psychoanalyst and philosopher in 2007 during the event "Carpi, the places of the word. The Words of the Gods". Hillman retrieves Renaissance philosophy and Greek mythology in his many texts.

There is one thing you learned before the others, jeans after jeans, jacket after jacket, down to the classic of classics, the blazer. A trivial but extremely useful thing: In business, the statement "Be yourself and you'll be fine" is out of context and totally lacking in business sense.

In business, form is substance.

Let's face it frankly: no one can afford to be a Steve Jobs and show up in a black turtleneck because there is no one like Steve Jobs[49].

I have known, in fact, managers who for a long time wore the Jobsian turtleneck but, believe me, they did not live up to that choker.

On important occasions, at meetings, at interviews, at conferences, as well as on first dates, the manager by chance knows that his fate is within eye contact, it is tied to the first impression.

A positive first impression not supported by facts is short-lived, but a negative first impression is worse. A negative first impression you never take away, like a sauce stain on a cotton blouse. No amount of bleach can take it away.

So if you want to be taken into consideration, you have to shape your professionalism. Find your look, express your personality while remembering that you are in a work environment.

No blue hair and Sailor Moon miniskirts or rocker looks, for that matter. An adult jacket and shoes are perfect for the corporate environment. Showing up at an important gathering in a sweatshirt, backpack and sneakers doesn't make you a transgressive original, it makes you out of context, unsuitable. If your thinking is brilliant you will certainly find a listen-

---

49 Steve Jobs' allegiance to black turtleneck sweaters finds explanation in the Apple guru's biography written by Walter Isaacson. Apparently, Jobs wanted to equip all his employees with a uniform, an idea that the Apple people did not like. Jobs then opted for a "leader's uniform", which he commissioned from designer Issey Miyake. With the black turtleneck, it was love.

ing ear, but the perception will remain in the onlookers that you are not environmentally homologous, reliable, mature.

This is the mistake made by the Peter Pan manager, the one who feels like a kid all the time, the one who does not want to compromise because he is different, he is other, he is better. A few weeks later you also discover him pandering to the follies of the Great Dictator, wearing sneakers all the time.

Wasn't it better to indulge him in a jacket?

Then there is the Chanel manager. The Chanel manager shines his own light. Whether man or woman or transgender, the first time you see him he dazzles you with excess of style and elegance of demeanor. Always impeccable, relentlessly name brand and fashionable, he exceeds in garment choices that you would wear to a wedding or for a New Year's Eve in style.

If woman, the Chanel manager wears only and exclusively Manolo shoes, as if she had freshly stepped out of the finer episodes of *Sex and the City*[50].

If male, he has the most beautifully tailored suit and cuffs you've ever seen. It's not uncommon for him to wear perfect shirts bordered exclusively with his own initials.

At first you can't help but label the Chanel manager[51] as out of place. Too chic, too elegant, too much. Yet, like all beautiful things, day after day its light seduces you and you find yourself in the morning in front of your wardrobe wondering what you can wear to give off a little bit of light yourself.

The Chanel manager, to give credit where credit is due, is the real person responsible for the company's dress education. Where he passes, fashion and good taste follow.

---

50 Cult television series from the 1990s, based on the novel by Candace Bushnell, which aired between 1998 and 2004, was followed by two feature films and in 2021 the sequel *And just like that*.
51 Coco Chanel (1883-1971) is the French fashion designer who revolutionized the concept of femininity, launching the fashion of short hair and elegance free in movement, for working, dynamic and autonomous women, even in pants.

Meetings turn into catwalks, speeches into diction lessons, walks into seduction. Bodies swaying admirably wrapped in fine garments like precious sarcophagi of refined minds: this is what they tell you as they walk down the corridors.

Superior beings, Chanel managers eat with each other as if they were the quintessence of etiquette, chatting with terms straight out of the poems of Dolce Stilnovo[52] but not lacking in generosity, opening up to others from time to time in the cafeteria area to spread their scent of spring, strawberries and roses over everyone.

And when it is casual friday[53], their performances of softness are unparalleled. You also remember on other days of the week the fluffiness of their cashmere on strictly designer jeans and eagerly wait to discover new looks.

You don't know if the Chanel manager is a good manager, you just love him.

---

52 From Guido Guinizelli, the Stilnovo influenced part of Italian poetry up to Francesco Petrarch, via Dante Alighieri. It revolves around the concept of pure love inspired by angelic women, which elevates men to their highest degree.
53 Casual friday is a recent American tradition that leads managers to indulge in a less formal style of dress at the office every Friday.

The Nerdy Manager

> *The world is full of obvious things that no one ever takes the trouble to observe.*
> Arthur Conan Doyle[54]

He is the nicest manager, the most bespectacled, the sharpest. He is the Nerdy manager. Everyone in the company has a soft spot for him. A hound of the impossible number, he lives between analytics and KPI, speaks in pivots and talks only through macros. You discover him in the office with his posture arched over the PC as if they constitute a whole, as if he has emerged from the myth of the two halves described in Plato's *Symposium*[55]. Once man and woman were one, perfect and beautiful, but Zeus, envious, divided them into two and destined them to search for each other all their lives. He did the same with Nerds and pc screens. He dresses casually, meaning he wears garments totally casually, grabbing them in the early morning dark, and lives on canned tuna and thought.

In the evening, having divested himself of the office Nerd, he dons those of the leisure Nerd. Swallowing tuna straight out of the can, he connects, beer in hand, with his other Nerd friends in online role-playing games, solutions to intriguing puzzles on video games born especially for him, or in endless dichotomous analyses of non-fungible tokens[56] and state-of-the-art algorithms vivisected by the Nerd's scalpel.

---

54 The phrase is from *The Hound of the Baskervilles* from 1902, Conan Doyle's third novel starring the detective Sherlock Holmes.
55 The *Symposium*, also known as the Convivio, is Plato's dialogue on the theory of love. The myth of the androgyne alluded to is given to Aristophanes.
56 Non-fungible tokens are deeds of ownership and cryptographic certificates of authenticity of an asset written on Blockchain. The digital art sector was the first to use NFTs, with significant quotations. Unlike cryptocurrencies, such as bitcoin, NFTs are not interchangeable.

Always a fan of comic books, always a lover of the fantasy genre, always a lover of science fiction, always a collector of collectables - necklaces, medals, pins, gadgets, rings -, the food processor that makes his milkshakes in the morning is named Darth Vader[57], because of the tapered, black figure and the metallic noise that comes from turning it on, and he considers The Hobbit[58] his best friend.

A lover of home automation, he does not turn on lights but operates them via apps and manages home devices with synthesizing tools of his own invention that Alexa gives them a run for their money. Loves voice assistants. He goes crazy over inventions. He's crazy about science crossword puzzles and listens to in-depth podcasts on his lunch break.

His favorite movie is *Blade Runner*[59], his preferred series is *Battlestar Galactica*[60], his music of choice is electronic music. An avid fan of David Bowie and Elon Musk[61], he eagerly experienced the launch of Perseverance to Mars, connecting in unison with other Nerds during the live broadcast from the Nasa website.

Not infrequently beneath the analytical manager's plaid sweatshirt beats a green heart: he comes to work on his bike

---

[57] Also known as Darth Vader or Lord Vader, he is the villain of villains in the *Star Wars* sci-fi saga.

[58] Hobbits are a race of minute men, inhabitants of Arda, the fictional land of setting of Tolkien's novels. From the book *The Hobbit* (1937), New Zealand director Peter Jackson made a film trilogy of the same name, in theaters in 2012, 2013 and 2014.

[59] A masterpiece of science fiction filmography directed by Ridley Scott in 1982, *Blade Runner* is loosely based on *Do Androids Dream of Electric Sheep?*, the 1968 novel by Philip K. Dick. In 2017, director Denis Villeneuve signed the remake *Blade Runner 2049*. Three prequel shorts followed: *2036: Nexus Dawn*, *2048: Nowhere To Run*, *Blade Runner: Black Out 2022*, the first two directed by Luke Scott, the last by Shin'ichirō Watanabe.

[60] Science fiction series created by Ronald D. Moore as a remake of the 1979 *Galactica* series.

[61] Strange coincidences. White Duke Bowie recorded *Life on Mars* in 1973 and in 2006 he played the character of Tesla in Christopher Nolan's film *The Prestige*. Elon Musk named his e-mobility company Tesla and with the aerospace company Space X aims to conquer Mars.

and helmet, is an expert on recycling, can't stand waste, and boasts a trained green thumb, growing pea seedlings and wild malva on the one windowsill of the low-ceilinged studio apartment where he falls asleep in front of consoles and PCs every night.

Last of the romantics, he would surrender his best processor to make out with the adventurous Trinity,[62] bang the legendary Queen Lagherta,[63] marry the timeless Princess Leia[64] or Arwen,[65] Princess of the Elves. Which makes him or her a perpetual single.

Similar in every way to the characters in the successful series *The Big Bang Theory*,[66] the Nerd, whether man or woman, is as close to sensory autism as it gets. You can only enter his world if you use his universal key: cryptogram and alpha numeric systems.

A friend of all functions, he is looked upon with sympathy and admiration by just about everyone. So shy, so on his own, so complex in his mode of expression that you can only understand him if you have taken a course with Eega Beeva[67] in simultaneous Nerdese-world, world-Nerdese translation.

But the aspect we like most about him is his total anaffectivity for human beings and his close affection for things. The Nerd cares more about his models in Power Bi[68] than his

---

62 Trinity is the main female character in the *Matrix* trilogy and the recent *Matrix resurrections*, the films directed by the Wachowski sisters.
63 Queen of Sweden, appears in the ninth volume of the *Gesta Danorum* by the medieval Danish historian Saxo Grammaticus.
64 Princess Leia Organa of Alderaan is the senator and general in *Star Wars*, the film saga conceived by George Lucas. Actress Carrie Fisher dressed her role.
65 A character in Tolkien's *The Lord of the Rings* trilogy, Arwen is half elf. In Peter Jackson's film saga she was played by actress Liv Tyler. For allure and poise Arwen resembles the manager Chanel.
66 Hilarious American sitcom in twelve seasons, social dissection of the world of Nerds.
67 Telepathic enigmatic character from Walt Disney comics and mothball devourer.
68 It is an enterprise business intelligence system, produced by the company Microsoft.

brother, appreciates the veracity of a keyboard more than the smile of his neighbor, trusts mathematical calculation more than his mother. And that affection, that care, that respect for that specific object that allows him to explore the world, his world, made of numbers, algorithms and signs, that feeling is sincere.

We know that the Nerdy manager is a good manager, and even if he were not, we would still love him.

The Willy Wonka Manager[69]

Tell me what you eat and I'll tell you who you are.
Anthelme Brillat-Savarin[70]

For the manager by chance, Fonzies stand to winter as Kit Kat stands to spring.

Trained to the non-stop marathon of staying at the PC, which not even Gandhi with his sit-ins could do better, and an unbeatable champion of lunch-hopping, the manager makes the coffee machine his wishing lair.

A magical place where, at the trivial jingle of a coin, in zero time, he receives some corking junk that keeps him alive: from the most disgusting coffee there is, but powerfully effective, to the tea used in dish rinses in India, which has come to us by the power of globalization, to the most coveted item, the chocolate snack or potato chip.

You may perhaps think that if it were possible, this manager would opt for battery power or intravenous transfusion of nutrients, as long as it is lightning fast and does not distract him unduly from the object of his desires: the macros or the diagram on duty.

But it doesn't. This manager desperately seeks a way out in sugar and salt, an effective compensation to total frustration, a flicker of chili pepper distraction, an escape to grueling meetings, a stage for shriveled egos seeking revenge, or escape from yet another office neighbor's rant.

---

69 *Willy Wonka & the Chocolate Factory* is a novel by Roald Dahl. Mel Stuart made a hit film from it in 1971, starring a terrific Gene Wilder, and director Tim Burton made a remake in 2005 starring Johnny Depp.
70 French gastronome who lived at the turn of the 18th and 19th centuries. He wrote *The Physiology of Taste*, which boasted a preface by Honoré de Balzac.

This manager needs all the junk. Of that sweetness that rises to the brain and tells you "it's all right", of that plastic taste that promises refreshment, of that salty frenzy that runs deep in the veins to the point of grogginess. So you don't know where you are, and if you get an inkling you can always take one last bite of the caramel snack, your dentist's delight.

In my company it is not like that. In my company they have decided to save our lives and remove any paid junk food dispensers placed in the area. They have invested in us and want us healthy and conscious, all day and forever. In return they provide us with fresh **Zero KM** fruit and organic whole grain crackers every day. They want us full, but light, proactive to the problem and effective in response.

The day they removed the cuddly machines on the Corporate Teams we all started using the hashtag #neveranyjoy.

Then again, there is always the evening, the homecoming, whatever time you get there. The moment when you cross the threshold, put down your purse, briefcase and overcoat, take off your shoes and after a quick run to the bathroom you dash into the kitchen, even before you've fed the cat and, greeting husband and canary, open the refrigerator and find nothing there. Nothing except a few parmesan cheese crusts you keep for superstition, dried up parsley from three weeks ago, and half a banana.

You will open the refrigerator and its echo will rumble through the empty shelves, orphaned of even the last tofu or soy steak. You will open the refrigerator and in your mind's eye you will visualize the Just Eat app, like the day before and the day before that. The delivery man who feeds you every night looks at you with a mixture of contempt and pity. You honestly don't care and ravenously lay the conquered dishes on the placemats as they arrive.

If you can put up with being a manager by chance, you can also accept that you didn't do the shopping.

Grocery shopping for the manager by chance is a matter

of organization, timing and methods in a drive for optimization at every scan.

Armed with little time, this manager hates the idea of queuing, queuing, waiting. It's not for him. This manager arranges online shopping with home delivery, delegates trusted people or points to the usual supermarket, where he knows orders and shelves by heart, to pick up what is needed for weekly survival: canned foods, precooked foods, pre-washed bagged salads, frozen pizzas and lots and lots of chocolate (see above).

A course of action that has very few exceptions: the manager with offspring to whose list must be added diapers, baby food, brains and peas, chips and coke; and the health manager.

The health manager aims to produce eternally with vigor and strength and abhors disease, with that note of hypochondriac superhomism that has always distinguished him. You recognize him immediately. He washes his hands all the time, keeps his proper distance, gets up at 5 a.m. for the usual early morning run, and if you clear your throat during a meeting he changes rooms and leaves the meeting. Without any warning. There, the health manager carefully selects ingredients, makes judicious purchases, and if he or she uses Just Eat takes only organic foods or dishes from macrobiotic restaurants.

Apart from the health manager and the manager with offspring, or especially in their case, the manager's grocery shopping is the litmus test of the state of neoliberal slavery in which he finds himself harnessed, where his narcissistic, performance-driven ego does not even allow him to get lost in the shelves, have a chat with the cashier, read the ingredients.

Even grocery shopping translates into an obstacle race-others and their carts-against time, to focus on his lifelong goal: corporate mega-production, an escape to the horror vacui of his existence.

The Vulcan Manager

> *I love the smell of napalm in the morning.*
>
> Colonel Bill Kilgore[71]

It is a sight you never want to witness, the erupting manager. It happens suddenly when you least expect it.

Something in the conversation, in the posture, in the atmospheric environment triggers in him the sudden scream, the aggression, the vituperation, the *j'accuse*[72], the quivering of the whole body, as if dominated by an epileptic seizure or in need of an exorcism.

Only he does not faint. Rather he continues, undaunted, to scream at you. To you who at that very moment, while the other colleague was talking, were thinking about something else, about the load of laundry to do in the evening, about the barley and spelt soup you are going to make for dinner, about how stubbornly refractory your youngest son proves to be about equations, about the latest Susan Bier[73] movie. You who, to the erupting manager have always shown sympathy, at least not rancor, not aversion. Perhaps a healthy safe distance.

But let's go step by step.

The Vulcan manager tends to be vivacious, bright, smiling, quick-witted. He is characterized by a nervous proxemics, an

---

[71] The phrase is from Francis Ford Coppola's film *Apocalypse now* (1979), loosely based on Joseph Conrad's *Hearts of Darkness* and set during the Vietnam War.

[72] Frenchman Emile Zola wrote this in 1898 in the socialist newspaper "L'Aurore". The "J'accuse" was addressed to Félix Faure, president of the French Republic. The episode was captured by director Roman Polansky in the 2019 film *The Officer and the Spy*, based on Robert Harris's novel *J'accuse*.

[73] Talented Danish filmmaker.

energetic walk with quick, close steps as well as a beating dialectic and dynamic speech that takes your breath away. A sort of Neapolitan Woody Allen following scripts written for him by Amy Sherman-Palladino, in one of the most intellectually hilarious episodes of *Gilmore Girls*, *The Marvelous Mrs. Maisel*[74] but in the set of *Pretend it's a City*[75] with Fran Lebowitz and Martin Scorsese: smart one-liners galore.

Most Vulcan managers are aesthetically inclined and manifest uncommon artistic gifts: musician, composer, painter, oftentimes sculptor, jewelry and design object creator. Their passion for beauty is reflected in fashionable clothing and attention to detail.

Although they share good taste, the Vulcan manager is clearly distinguished from the Chanel manager by less measured management of space and frenzy of movement.

A Chanel would never burst into a room, never adopt quick movements. The Chanel manager is class and elegance, thoughtful slowness. The Vulcan manager is Sturm und Drang,[76] impetus and passion. Vulcan is creativity.

You adore the vulcanic manager on good days, he brings good cheer to the office, he bursts into your meetings with a joke, he stuns you with his likability, his overwhelming smile and the unmistakable ring of his laughter that, emitted on the ground floor, you hear on the fourth floor behind closed doors.

Then, from time to time, something goes wrong, something in her jests runs aground. A twisted, devious thought grafts itself into his sunny disposition, and the jokester turns

---

74 *Gilmore girls* and *The Marvelous Mrs. Maisel* are two TV series created by Amy Sherman Palladino characterized by well-constructed dialogue and sharp, quotable, and tight dialectics.

75 The Netflix-signed documentary series chronicles the New York City writer and actress Fran Lebowitz as she is interviewed by her friend Martin Scorsese.

76 German cultural movement, the Sturm und Drang, literally storm and rush, contributed to the birth of Germanic Romanticism, between 1765 and 1785.

into an unstoppable angry hyena with gushes of venom that pierce your heart if you've given him confidence on happy days.

In those moments there is no logic involved. Responding to him in kind increases the corrosive lava; defending yourself does worse. The only viable practice is to wait for the eruption to end and in the meantime duck to avoid pyroclastic flow and mudslides.

Beware of confusion.

The Vulcan manager and the incontinent manager are brothers in fits of rage, fellow rants, honorary members of the same competitive family, yet they are not the same manager. The incontinent one makes the uncontained expression of his feelings his stylistic hallmark, which he maintains with firm consistency by reiterating his behavior every day.

In contrast, unpredictability characterizes the Vulcan manager. He could sit quietly for months and months, for years even, and suddenly detonate for no apparent reason. The incontinent manager is forever, Vulcan surprises you. The incontinent manager works on constancy, the Vulcan on power.

One thing is certain. At the first sudden eruption and without warning you understand that behind that smile, behind that joke, behind that always sympathetically upbeat being lies a magma of complexity that not even Freud could explain.

You realize this and try not to be caught unprepared the next time. You arm yourself with an umbrella, as the inhabitants of Gravina di Catania do to protect themselves from the falling ash of Mount Etna, you practice, eruption after eruption, to recognize the first signs of telluric landslides and retreat in time.

Sooner or later, in spite of all your precautions, you will catch another eruption, but you will be less and less surprised, you will be less and less stupefied, more and more awake and quicker to take cover.

And those eruptions will become habitual, moments of the day, episodes to which you will have become accustomed. As the inhabitants of the towns of Etna get used to how their god Vulcan communicates.[77]

---

[77] He is the Roman god of fire, known for his creative and, at the same time, destructive tendencies. His counterpart in Greek mythology is Hephaestus. Often depicted as a blacksmith, he created imposing objects and precious jewelry with the use of fire. It is no coincidence that the manager vulcanic is known not only for his unexpected eruptions but also for his brilliant creative talents and passion for accessories and costume jewelry that he often makes himself.

The Geeky Manager

> *I don't know what's wrong with me, says Marianne. I don't know why I can't be like normal people.*
> Sally Rooney[78]

He's been at the top of the class since first grade, which I say: since kindergarten. He wears his pinafore as proudly as a marine wears his uniform at the ship's launch parade where he will soon be named admiral. Never frayed, never crumpled, embellished, taut, as taut is his attention to every single word issued by the teacher.

Champion of the cleanest pinafore of the year every year and first in the league in organizing the snack basket, he prefers the company of adults to that of his peers, focused on grasping the secrets of adulthood.

Inclined from the cradle not to waste time on games devoid of productivity, performance and achievement are important to him.

If he has to play with musical carousels or the spinning mobile, he does so by emitting perfect symphonies. If he works with Legos, he doesn't devolve until the Elsinore castle[79] is complete.

Allergic to stuffed animals, he prefers games with mechanisms and puzzles to solve and quizzes, where he engages until he wins. It goes without saying that "The Chemistry Lab" has no formulaic secrets for him.

---

78 The sentence is from *Normal People*, the Irish author's 2019 work, which followed *Conversation with friends* in 2018. From *Normal People* is the TV series of the same name set to air in 2020.
79 Elsinore Castle, originally Kronborg Castle, a fortress located in Helsingor, Denmark, is the setting for William Shakespeare's tragedy *Hamlet*.

Precocious in reading, precocious in addition, precocious enough, he routs the competition by arousing two controversial feelings in children his age and their parents: admiration and rancor.

Fundamental humus for his growth is loneliness, to which he is condemned despite his saccharine and assertive behavior. Rejected by others, he repeatedly closes himself behind one book and then another and then another until he builds up a personal library of eight thousand volumes, arranged in Ikea shelving units on two perfectly parallel rows and planes.

Dating back to middle school is the encounter with other scattered geeks from other sections, the initial envy, the hostility to excel, and finally the solidarity of the outsider who finds in the readers' club, the chess group, and the school newspaper editorial staff a place to belong.

Other geeks fare better. They understand from a young age the inestimable value in the school market of those who hold the knowledge and the chance of a good grade and voluntarily permute completed assignments and test papers in exchange for smiles, outings to the movies and sometimes a smidgen of friendship or a snack. They are the extroverted geeks, a different kettle of fish than the pure geeks, more sociable, more approachable, with a relational approach that combined with commitment makes all the difference in business.

Even in adulthood, the geek is obviously a victim of himself and the first-in-class syndrome. If he does not stand out, if he does not emerge, if he is not the best he inexorably suffers the pains of hell and goes into depression.

In the best cases of failure he perseveres with the same determination with which Annie Wilkes cares for Paul Sheldon in *Misery Must Not Die*[80] until he finds a solution and emerges like the Phoenix from its own ashes.

---

80 Based on the novel *Misery* by Stephen King, the film directed by Rob Reiner in 1990 earned Kathy Bates, playing the psychopathic Annie Wilkes, an Oscar and a Golden Globe for Best Actress in a Motion Picture Drama.

The will of the geeky manager is ironclad, at the expense of even physical health, mental health, leisure time and private relationships. And of vacations, holidays, Christmas and bank holidays. Also characterizing him in the office is a drive for continuing education, tireless study, the pursuit of in-depth study to the point of neuronal exhaustion. His resumes even at a young age are three pages long, two of them populated with rows of masters, semi-masters, training courses, webinars, tutorials and internships that even an academic cannot boast of.

But if these aspects elude you in assessing the geeky manager, there are other idiosyncratic characteristics that cannot go unnoticed.

The geeky manager has a physiological and existential need to always, and I mean always, express his or her opinion. Even when it is not required. Once expressed, he quiets down and returns to his desk, silent and focused. A relay goal achiever with triple pike leap, a problem solver by exercise, he feels he is not being fair to those who hired him if he does not expound his intelligence under all circumstances.

It is not enough for him to share his thinking, he must do so in great detail, delving into assumptions that perhaps the audience already knows, into pleonastic and redundant but accurate explanations.

The geeky manager can't help himself. He cannot fail to spend your time in elucidating the genesis of Hebrew script from the tablets of Moses to the script of *Unorthodox*[81] or clarifying for you what it means to conjugate the subjunctive today, the intrinsic value of hedge pruning to contemporary society or the scientific differentiation between solar panels and photovoltaic panels.

If it doesn't it implodes. Psychosomatic illnesses such as

---

81 A Netflix signature TV series, Maria Shrader's *Unorthodox* tells the story of a courageous Brooklyn Jewess who escapes to Berlin to build an existence as a woman independent of the stringent Chassidic traditions.

GCC, gastritis, cystitis and colitis, are as friendly to him as Donald Duck is to his cape, and they come out copious and strong in a state of great dictatorship, in situations in which the geeky manager cannot constitutionally give his best.

The geeky manager has an extremely high rate of touchiness in his body, as if he had downed five bottles of "I know".

Interrupting him, not understanding him, or questioning his scholarly and professional competence hurts him to the core. To objections he reacts by stiffening and using sharp and unparalleled logic with the flick of his tail, which never leaves him, openly marking his superiority over the oppressor.

Interlocutors find it convenient to dismiss the episode as a case of frayed ego rigidity before even understanding what actually occurred.

We would be unfair if we dismissed the geek's dialectical and thinking ability in such an overused word as "susceptibility". Conversely, we would be wrong if we did not discern in him a massive and abundant dose of self-love.

TThe key is to fully understand that he is neither egoistic or narcissistic, but all-consuming: the geeky manager forces himself to perform at his best to the point of exhaustion. When he feels he has not, hedives deep into exhausting, superfluous excuses and explanations, to himself before to others.

Having his support is easier than peeling an orange. Just ask him for help.

Deep down the geeky manager has no ambition to manifest his intellectual superiority. He simply loves to express his knowledge, to barter what he knows in exchange for your friendship.

The Designer Manager

> *Early in life I had to choose between honest arrogance and hypocritical humility. I chose the former and have seen no reason to change.*
>
> Frank Lloyd Wright[82]

He used to be called a graphic designer or creative. What a platitude. Today it is copywriter, SEO copywriter, web copywriter, social media manager, content manager, storyteller, graphic designer, fashion designer, web designer, emotional designer, product designer, design thinker, and much more.

Presumptuous to summarize in one list the magical and multiplying world of today's creatives. What we can say with confidence and the justice is that whatever list we draw up will be topped by him and only him, the art director, the god of graphic design, the authority on the subject.

If you have one in your company, you recognize him immediately. Stylish to a fault, he wears color, fabric, and fashion era combinations that would make anyone else look like an unlikely cross between Queen Elizabeth and Britney Spears, with accusations of indecent behavior raining down.

He doesn't. He can afford the juxtaposition of double-colored sneakers, bow tie and suspenders, he can dare a plaid skort with a tunic and look cool, he can use an old overcoat and not be compared to Lieutenant Columbo,[83] he can associate rococo style with puffed sleeves and metal leather pants from the 1980s. The total black turtleneck pull-

---

82 Architect who shaped the history of 20th-century American urban planning.
83 The legendary Lieutenant Columbo is the protagonist of the television detective series *Columbo*, which aired between 1968 and 2003 and starred actor Peter Falk.

over jacket is one of his must-haves, as are khaki suits of various shades, which give him a soft appearance and emphasize his curvaceous figure.

The Pantone color booklet dominates his desk, as well as a set of perfectly sharpened pencils, a few industry publications, a few of his own, an endless sequence of books from Taschen, and a few over-the-top and important recognition plaques handed out by the ADC Awards or some other over-the-top and important association.

If you delve deeper you will understand that he is a master in the field. An expert in aesthetics, history of art and advertising, a linguist by academic study, he detests trivialization and will nail you down for an hour detailing every single detail, the importance of typographic choice, the need for reflection on the type of paper, the distinctions between one the balances between the parts, the right pantones, the correct context, the meaning and signifier, the chrisms of communication, the lettering, the beginnings of advertising, the discrepancy of the dot on the i in the claim that goes to interfere dangerously with the image of the hot air balloon in the upcoming advert.

And you, who hadn't even considered that dot, intent on grasping the whole, feel like you're in an episode of Mad Men but without Don Draper[84], the whiskey by the bucketful, rarely diluted with ice, and the smoke in the room you could cut with an axe.

The art director flaunts superiority, and we don't begrudge him that. In terms of image and communication culture, his

---

84 Don Draper is the charming publicist who stars in the cult television series *Mad Men* created by Matthew Weiner and set in 1960s New York City. The series, produced from 2007 to 2015, reconstructs the dynamic world of American advertising in those years. Mad men is the epithet by which advertising creatives who worked on Madison Avenue were identified. In 2013, the Taschen publishing house published two splendid volumes *Advertising for the Mad men era*, a collection of ads from the 1950s and 1960s, a must-have cultural heritage for marketing managers and managerial designers.

primacy is genuine, backed by years of glorious experience, research and in-depth knowledge.

Sometimes it is complex to work with him. You try to explain the project to him, and he scans you from top to bottom, manifesting with raised eyebrow contempt for the plaid pants you wear in the morning, for the carelessness and superficiality you display toward images, for your total lack of knowledge. Let's face it: not easy.

It only gets worse if the art director is a veteran of the golden years of advertising, between the 1960s and 1980s, when his or her divinity was tangibly recognized on Earth.

In this specific case, digressions about the good times and trophies of the past take over. Always. The commercials he devised, the brands he supported, the actors he interfaced with, the composers he called on, the directors he worked with fit shamelessly into any kind of conversation, from what you had for dinner last night - "there was one time when Federico[85] decided to cook carbonara. It was awful [deep laughter betraying a past as a student of diction classes, reinforced by dreamy gaze over the wall and chin up, followed by a deep, serious frown, like a true thoughtful professional] - to how to enhance an advertising message in the context of a billboard - "At Leo Burnett we didn't do that. And we were right".

We would be unfair if we asserted with confidence that all the older creative professionals have these characteristics.

The art director, the good one, is at his best when he makes his knowledge available to others, when he shares his knowledge with an audience of enraptured and admiring disciples, when he takes you to a biennial.

If you know him you don't avoid him. If you know him you follow him.

---

85 I imagine the designer manager alludes to Federico Fellini.

The Structured Manager

> *Jerome had been engineered with everything he needed to get into Gattaca, except the desire to do so.*
>
> Vincent Freeman[86]

The manager who works in multinational companies is something else. A separate chapter must obligatorily be devoted to him, starting with the assumption of assumptions: managerial theory has constructed the dogma of the manager as the key to professional management in the modern corporation. And we, who are managers, believe in that dogma.

While manager by chance grapples in the entropy of SMEs or family-run businesses, striving every day for clarity of roles, clarity of projects, clarity of communications with a few too many thoughts about euthanasia over the weekend, the multinational manager has none of these problems.

He lives in a structured and organized world where he doesn't have to win his space, doesn't have to draw his fence, doesn't have to struggle every day with insane and unproductive overlaps, doesn't have to be a gladiator.

He arrives at the company as fresh as his laundry and takes his place. It is there waiting for him, made explicit in its boundaries, with its tasks, with the bricks already placed in predefined order, boundaries invisible to outsiders but very clear within the company organization. A little square of his own.

He does not have to scramble to understand, does not have to engineer to act and expand, does not have to brush

---

[86] Freeman stars in *Gattaca*, a 1997 sci-fi film starring Ethan Hawke, Uma Thurman and Jude Law.

up on Spartan techniques of defense in a Roman conflict. He belongs there. He simply has to do his best inside that enclosure in the eight hours that mark his workday.

Relaxing, isn't it? Just know how to do your job, not one skill more not one skill less, and that's it. Eight hours of work, exactly. Not eight hours and fifteen minutes, not ten, not twelve.

Your evenings are saved, your weekends are free. You can walk the dog, sleep eight hours a night, play with your children, cook, engage in gardening, read all the spy stories you can think of, make love, go to the movies, attend a rock concert and hide out in a museum, have a blast with your watercolors and become the wizard of DIY. The quality of your life is back. It is all yours; you are saved.

Yet, looking at it as a whole, even that little square has its pitfalls. You quickly learn that you can snack with whomever you want, smile at colleagues in the other function, share how your weekend went. Go ahead and socialize, but remember to be careful. Because behind those multinational smiles lies a world of sharks, animals known for their aggression and ferocity but underestimated in terms of social dynamics. They often roam in packs and are very supportive of each other.

That little square that at first glance seems so reassuring therefore has its own rules. It is vital not to overstep its boundaries, even to get a breath of air. Taking a peek at the neighboring square is a risk, a highly dangerous game where the solidity of your position is at stake. If you do so, you must act with the utmost caution.

Curiosity killed the cat.

In this complicated game of boundaries and diplomacy, in this web of unspokenness, refined dissimulation is also essential. In short, don't make explicit to others what is occurring in your own backyard if you don't want the boss to toss you out, unless it is a tactic that has been worked out with your team.

In multinational corporations, more powerfully than in smaller companies, you are a square on a massive chessboard, a cog in a mammoth machine. If you don't immediately understand where you are, what your little place is, who to team up with, you're screwed. The organization engulfs you as if you were a gnat.

Having made it clear that SMEs[87] and multinationals differ substantially in layout, game dynamics and underlying philosophy-in multinationals, form is everything, always-and thus defined the manager's space, its relationship to the other coordinate in our Cartesian system, time, must be understood.

In multinationals, the timelines for go-to-market or project grounding are infinitely longer than in smaller companies.

Every decision involves the involvement of other populous business functions, in-depth reflections, relaunching in subsequent meetings, re-balancing, going back on previous bets, lunging at future ones. Hierarchical transitions from level to level as in a PlayStation game, with the rather high probability of pressing the wrong button and going back, as in snakes and ladders.

Every single step this manager takes, is part of the whole corporate structure, stable and secure and with important specific weight, which makes him slow down in his movements.

The multinational manager is not a 100-meter runner; he does not play fast sprints.

Rather, he is a marathon runner, patient, steady, accurate, careful about where he puts his foot. For it is a moment to stumble.

The play of parts, the direct confrontation he was used to in smaller companies, is played out here on a higher level. It's clash of functions, it's teamwork, it's fighting between packs of sharks. It is unspoken. You don't go wrestling anymore, you play volleyball. You engage in a higher game, wearing white gala gloves, you're not supposed to get your hands dirty.

---

87   Acronym for small and medium-sized enterprises.

The structured manager always walks as if he's shoehorning Dr. Martens and wearing a tuxedo, feet firmly clamped to the ground, posture erect and looking at the nearby square, careful not to step on its edges and ready to win the game over time, along with the other ball guests like him.

The Enlightened Manager

> *I've seen things you people wouldn't believe. Attack ships on fire off the shoulder of Orion. I watched C-beams glitter in the dark near the Tannhäuser Gate. All those moments will be lost in time, like tears in rain.*
>
> Roy Batty[88]

It is rumored to be a rumor, a mythopoetic tale in corporate fiction, a dream, a chimera, a manager's mirage.

Yet the enlightened manager exists. The enlightened manager is.

A dying breed, a veteran of collapsing situations and verbal assaults at gunpoint that are bitterly part of corporate life cycles, the enlightened manager is distinguished by his manners: well-mannered, polite, never disheveled, with a calm tone of voice, never hysterical, an absolute lack of improper language, banned for life from his vocabulary.

The enlightened manager is the quintessential gentleman, somewhere between a lord and a member of the Accademia della crusca. He never disrespects you, listens carefully, welcomes your mistakes and does not judge you for them.

With him in view if a project has errors and shortcomings it is the wrong project to be remedied, not you an imbecile, a manager not up to his role who does not make peace with his brain.

---

[88] The phrase is from *Blade Runner* the Ridley Scott masterpiece. There are seven versions of the feature film, from the 1982 original to 2007's *The Final Cut* via 1992's *The Director's Cut*. In each appears the statement of the replicant Roy, on the verge of death, declaimed by actor Rutger Hauer.

The enlightened one is focused on the what and not the who, on the goal, not the person.

The enlightened one knows what it means to have a "culture of error", the ability to learn from one's mistakes and the mistakes of others in order to improve together in an agile approach toward continuous progress.

Working with him is like being in Lorenzo de Medici's[89] court, a spectator and actor in a new era, a new Renaissance, where people are valued and pushed to give their best.

A born motivator, he rarely fails to receive applause and sincere approval. For him you are willing to work late into the evenings, revise your business plan over the weekend, redo your simulations several times to make sure you don't flake out and get a chance to be able to support him. And you do this with a lightness in your heart and with only the desire that the enlightened one reciprocate your affection and admiration.

With the enlightened one, in short, it is love. Not only because of the natural and physiological care the enlightened one manifests toward you, but also because of the deep preparation he expresses daily by working hard beside you until late.

The enlightened person embodies Simon Sinek's *Leaders Eat Last*[90] volume, word for word. He is the first one in the office and the last one out. If the project goes well, it is thanks to the teamwork, with which he shares awards and recognition. If something goes wrong, the responsibility is his.

With him you feel supported, covered, safe. Having him as a mentor changes your professional career, marks your destiny as a good person in business, opens you wide to a future

---

89 Called the Magnificent, Lorenzo de Medici was lord of Florence from 1469 until his death. A proponent of the Renaissance, a humanist prince, he represents in all respects the prototype of the enlightened manager.

90 Translated as "Last Comes the Leader", *Leaders Eat Last* is a work by marketing guru Simon Sinek, father of the golden circle and the power of why.

of competence and intellectual honesty, leads you to follow in his footsteps and work like him every day for the common good, for the prosperity of the community and the health of the world. With him the relationship is sustainable, it is factually *human to human*[91]. In front of him you stand stripped of all the trappings of corporate advocacy, the unsubstantiated forms, the appearances, the postures of showmanship. It is you, there, naked with all your ambitions and insecurities, with all your humanity.

Aggravating an enlightened one is rare but possible. Above all, it is a road of no return. The enlightened manager has a Sai Baba-like patience, an above-average threshold of endurance, somewhat like Superman's endurance to pain. Exceeding that threshold means no more chance with him; it means hitting you with kryptonite.

The enlightened one must therefore be handled with care. With the enlightened one you can be yourself but you cannot fool him with simulation, ostentation, deception and professional fraud. In that case it is over for you.

The enlightened one exists. But he is not forever. When you meet him, acknowledge him and thank your lucky stars. Capitalize on your experience with him as much as possible, be grateful for his existence.

If you behave well, if you are sincere, if you are honest you will find that an enlightened manager will remain in your life even years later. He will remain in your heart, he will remain in the teachings of generosity he has given you.

Meeting an enlightened manager is a rare event. When it happens, it is your lucky day.

---

[91] The concept of *human to human* was introduced by marketing daddy Philip Kotler in 2017 by talking about sustainable marketing and scratching the previous distinctions between *business to business* and *business to consumer*.

LIFE AS A MANAGER

A Leader is not Denied to Anyone

Once there were the great leaders, the kings, the Charlemagne, the Frederick II, the Stalin, the Lenin, the Roosevelt, the Churchill. And the Arthurian kings, the Lancelots, the Lears, the Augustuses, and the Vercingetorixes. And, more recently, the Obamas, the Clintons, the Reagans, the Gorbachevs, the Mitterands.

They were fighting battles, imposing actions, leading, fearless, toward victory, obliging, determining, demanding, deciding, not backing down. You followed them to the ends of the earth just because they said so.

You risked your life for your king and what he stood for: land, freedom from the invader, religious belief, political faith, gold, hunger, thirst, sleep.

You did it, and if you succeeded, you received a guarantee in return: the reassurance of having a roof over your head, food for your children, and a few coins.

Today things have changed, but not that much. They have slipped, slid, declined, changed semantic field. So would say the SEO[92] expert who works with us managers by chance every day.

Today there are no kings and leaders. You look for them among TV gurus, among Instagram influencers[93], among Hol-

---
92 Search engine optimization involves a set of activities to optimize a website to improve its ranking in the non-paid (organic) results of search engines such as Google.
93 Influencer marketing is a branch of marketing that has never more than in recent years taken over certain market segments, such as, for example, youth fashion. Some influencers have made an empire out of it. A topic for discussion. Market studies claim that 92 percent of consumers believe in people's recommendations and reviews more than in brand commu-

lywood stars and on high-fashion runways. You no longer follow them in armed war campaigns but on their social pages. You don't arm yourself with swords but with likes, you don't hail them, you share them, in a viral process that pays no mind to geographic boundaries, religious beliefs, gender and lineage.

Sometimes, you don't want to, but you find them, despite yourself, in your company. In those companies where the use of the term leadership is more widespread than grating parmesan cheese over macaroni.

There he is-the decision leader, the disciplinary leader, the motivational leader, the friendship leader, the demanding leader, the democratic leader, the visionary leader.

An army of leaders, one more qualified than the other, appealing to their call sign in the hope that you will follow them willingly. Leaders who are indistinguishable from one another, leaders who overlap, nominalistic leaders, leaders so populous in the company that there is no one left to follow. A "leader" is not denied to anyone.

It goes without saying that if you are not a leader nowadays, it is a big problem. But don't panic, it doesn't take much to be one. Just take a leadership course, even online.

Coaches will analyze you, test you, and teach you how to look inside yourself, clusters you, and choose from the leadership catalog what is right for you. Having identified which category you belong to, wearing your leader, like a suit, they put you through leadership and management courses, "designed

---

nications, seeking an authenticity of message and relationship that has faded in recent years. In the wake of this research, there is another phenomenon of interest. It is called *Employee brand advocacy* and involves the involvement of one's employees-true, real, honest brand ambassadors-in the communication dynamics to consumers and customers. It is a putting one's face on it and ensuring through the sincere gaze of those who work there every day the quality of the service and product they offer. It is an exposure that involves serious, substantial relationship and trust work with its employees. Otherwise it doesn't work. It is the present and the future of the company. It is the return to the person.

for those who manage people and responsibilities within modern organizations", reads one of the many brochures. In the course of the classes they explain to you how a real leader thinks, talks, eats, watches, listens, and goes to the toilet.

The leader's proxemics are different depending on what type of leader he or she belongs to.

The Democratic leader maintains equidistance from everyone, with a static smile on his face, always. Great equilibrist, diplomat by nature, he is the leader who confirms the Aristotelian theory of man as a political animal. With a pronounced sense of justice and inclusiveness, if he had not happened to be a manager in business, he would have undoubtedly become a judge, lawyer or social worker dedicated to integrating other peoples into our society. Zodiac sign: Libra.

The friendly leader is the one who tends to give you the classic pat on the back. From him you can expect frequent hugs. He is the leader who in the pandemic period manifested the most suffering. When the Ministry of Health recommended social distancing, he got sick. His favorite motto? "Let's team up!"

The visionary leader has erect bearing and a pronounced upward chin in a "I'm scanning the horizon" posture. It is said that one of his ancestors served as a lookout on the Santa Maria when Columbus discovered the Americas. He is the leader who tends to piss you off the most, because he visualizes a lot but materializes little.

The disciplinary leader orders all the pens on his desk every morning in a perfectly parallel fashion, serial killer model. Creating entropy in his space is impossible. A detail maniac, if you move an ornament he notices it as soon as he enters the room. An object out of place is for him a reason for existential suffering. His is a world of rules to follow. The disciplined leader is the one who most respects the corporate organization.

You immediately recognize the demanding leader: he often exposes the index finger of his right hand, or left hand if left-handed, in the air, pointing it generically at you. But he should not be misunderstood. The demanding leader is very demanding first and foremost of himself. He wakes up at 5 a.m. to jog and show up at the office before others perfectly focused. He skips his lunch break eating energy bars in front of the PC, leaves the office last. And he doesn't complain about it, ever. His secret: he can't stand the decision-making leader. He does not accept that someone else can make decisions for him.

The motivational leader always goes to lunch with the friendly leader and the demanding leader. He always tends to choose the seat in between the two, the demanding leader facing the window, the friendly leader facing the other tables. You'll find him busy priming his following with customized slogans, depending on the case, the type of employee, the circumstance, and the life cycle of the company. The motivational leader never gives up on you. Sometimes he even chases you into the bathroom and calls periodic team meetings with unlikely names, from "Ground Control to Major Tom"[94] to "Magnolia, where ideas flourish" to "Blade funnel". In the pandemic period, his drive for supportive encounters found chat platforms his most valuable ally. He was the first to understand how Zoom, Teams, and Google Meet worked, the first to find the background customization feature.

The decisive leader has long, plush strides if a man or close rhythmic cleats if a woman. You know it's him because he's outspoken, doesn't mince words, and above all, he stands out with determination. Acoustically, too. For the decisive leader, a no is never a no. It is simply a momentary obstacle that reinforces his "leadership-city.

We are all leaders. And you, what kind of leader are you?

---

94 This is a line from David Bowie's song *Space Oddity*, a single released in 1969, the year of man's landing on the moon. The song is among the five hundred songs that shaped rock and roll in the Rock and Roll Hall of Fame in Cleveland.

The Manager and ~~Free~~ Time

What is this, a joke?

The BOD Room

A company without a BOD room is not a self-respecting company.

An acronym - BOD - that can be variously interpreted.
Board Of Directors
Balls Of Dictators
Beauty Of Death
Better Or Die
Bastards On Board
Biscuits Of Devastation
And many more.

All acronyms that partly anticipate what happens in that room. Coveted by those outside it, feared by those inside, it looks like an episode of *Lost*[95] or Steven Spielberg's *The Twilight Zone*[96].

A nonplace where you know when you enter but you don't know when and how you'll leave. An (un)filtered place where everyone's dark side emerges tangibly and rarefies into the atmosphere, like consistent clouds laden with rainwater above us. Occasionally you get your own downpour, sometimes you suffer others' hail.

But the BOD hall does not lie; it betrays right from the furniture its essence. Most rooms run the length of the room with long black or lacquered glass tables and dark leather chairs.

---

[95] A cult series created in 2010 by Jeffrey Lieber, J.J. Abrams and Damon Lindelof, it catalyzed audience attention for six seasons. A must-read is *The Philosophy of Lost* by Simone Regazzoni, a student of Jacques Derrida and former author of *Pop filosofia* and *La filosofia di Harry Potter*.

[96] *The Twilight Zone* is a science fiction television series created by Rod Serling, scripted by Richard Matheson, Charles Beaumont and Ray Bradbury, broadcast from 1959 to 1964 with several reboots. In 1983 director Steven Spielberg signed a film of it together with colleagues John Landis, Joe Dante and George Miller.

At the head of the table is the executive, at the sides the managers in order of importance, all armed with baskets of candy, glasses and branded water jugs.

At the first meeting you immediately understand from the sessions the corporate hierarchical ladder or, at least, the ambitions of individual managers. There is the climber manager who positions himself behind the Father, the Pontius Pilate manager who deflects to the back, next to the Nerd, Cassandra in the middle position with Penelope, Willy Wonka on the way out with his thoughts on snacks and four bon-bon wrappers in his hands.

Conquering the chairs at the top is not easy. From proximity to the royal chair you also understand the power allocation of individual functions. If the sales manager is better positioned than the marketing manager, then you know the company is sales driven and that is where the power is concentrated. Vice versa if marketing has the best seat. If it is management control that approaches the top, there is none for anyone else. Operations often gets the top spot in telcos, manufacturing and R&D in companies where the product has a high scientific content, such as pharmaceutical companies.

It is an instructive place where, if you are a good observer, you understand the main movements of the chessboard and acquire a great deal of information that is very useful for your survival in the company.

BOD rooms are rarely bright. Often darkened to allow the projection of PowerPoint with company market and positioning data, sales figures, churn rates, marketing projects, industrial plans, they capitalize on the dark atmosphere to enhance its value and maintain the allure of secrecy. Sort of like the scene in *Mary Poppins*[97] where George Banks, upstanding

---

97 Surprisingly, the "Mary Poppins" manager, loosely based on the successful 1964 Disney feature film, does not peep into these pages. The Mary Poppins manager has a stern approach, wears flat shoes, has a resealable umbrella always with her and a weakness for licorice. Her mission is to train the informable and make them into business executives. Every

London banker, interfaces with the Board of the bank that is in financial crisis for two pennies.

In the darkness everything seems more reserved, more important, more powerful.

In that darkness when we find ourselves presenting projects, in the midst of debate with a colleague who expresses reticence, perplexity or animated opposition to our thinking, as in a large arena or sumo wrestling show, we feel a bit like Banks. In those moments we would like to remember that "when you have nothing to say, all you can say is... supercalifragilisticexpialidocious [98].

Do not underestimate the power of the BOD room. A power in its own right, independent of its inhabitants. A magical and diabolical place at the same time.

What really happens in there is known only by those four walls, lit by dim lights and adorned with corporate graphics, portraits of founders and executives, and artificial plants so refined they seem real.

Things happen in that room. You walk out of it taking only a piece of it with you. The rest of it stays there, like a Blob[99], an extraterrestrial being that at the next meeting will reabsorb your thoughts to make you take away another little piece.

And in the end there is a risk that inside that Blob is you too.

---

self-respecting accidental manager with a team to manage is a bit, at heart, a Mary Poppins manager. Sometimes you recognize him by the flowers he wears in his buttonhole, unlikely ties with stylized daisies or cactus-shaped earrings.

98 The phrase is from the film *Mary Poppins*, which won a Golden Globe and five Academy Awards in 1965, including the score by Richard and Robert Sherman and the Best Actress award for Julie Andrews.

99 *The Blob* is a 1958 science fiction horror film directed by German director Irving S. Yeaworth Jr, which was followed by a remake in 1988. The Blob is a shapeless, gelatinous extraterrestrial creature that tends toward phagocytosis of whatever object or being it encounters in its path.

"Meetingitis" Kills
Read the warnings carefully

They don't tell you so as not to scare you. You cross the corporate threshold for the first time and they don't tell you. They don't tell you that as time goes by and you presumably get ahead you will be engulfed by an osmotic system of meeting relays, session strings, calls, video calls, constraints, one after another until you too inexorably are overwhelmed and screwed by what is the real endemic evil of the corporate system: meetingitis.
A disease, an infection for which there is no antibiotic or vaccine that holds, a disease that becomes an existential status and from which you have no escape.

Meetingitis is one of the pandemics of the third millennium. You start as a junior getting involved in the gatherings, first as a discreet guest, then as a speaker. You are happy and proud when you win your place in the meeting, that quarter-hour of speaking time that is only the prelude to your ascent up the meeting hierarchy ladder, until you find yourself an active participant and meeting inducer, a proliferator of conjunctive bacilli, a spreader of meetingitic sperm, an insane and fertile carrier of disease.

"I'll send you a calendar". "I'll set you an appointment on Outlook". These are words that should chill you. Instead you are stolidly unaware of the trouble you have gotten yourself into. You're elated.

"At last I can call a meeting", you say playfully to yourself as, with a chest full of pride, you press the macchiato coffee button on the machine in the break area. It almost doesn't seem real to you. You call people into a meeting. Part triumphant, part tentative and you won't make it to lead that first meeting of yours, terrified that he will lead you.

We've all been there. A first deep breath and off you go: there you are, smiling in front of a gathering of colleagues, projecting your first slides. It's like riding a bicycle, you think. First you approach the road supported by the side wheels, then you proceed on two wheels, sometimes you fall, but if you get back up quickly, without others noticing, one day you will have the bike. One day. And you will speed like a train to new meetings. Maybe you will create an empire of them. An empire of meetings, one on top of the other, piled up in order like the floors of a fearless, ambitious skyscraper.

It is only after some time, after you have collected a significant number of meetings, those same meetings that, almost feverishly, you so yearned to attend, it is only after you have shaken off the enchantment that you have become a grown-up professional, complete with a meeting license, it is only then that you begin to grasp the exact essence of the meeting itself.

You thought it was convenient to share, communicate, compare, support, proceed, concretize.

You believed it for a while, with your whole self, even with the leather laptop backpack your parents gave you at graduation, even with the useless business card holder, even with the stapler and the paper basket.

You used to believe it, but now you can't help but see, catch that sad, real, tangible pattern underlying the meeting, underlying not one meeting but a thousand, not all but many meetings in the world.

Vanity. More than a few meetings have as their strategic assumption their exhibitionist essence, their show for show's sake, pure entertainment that justifies the presence of a kick-ass hourly mol[100] sitting around the same table.

---

[100] Gross operating margin, a profitability indicator that does not consider taxes, interest, depreciation and amortization of assets. Hourly mol indi-

Some meetings are a vanity fair.

Raise your hand if you have not endured half-hour monologues by managers who meticulously expound every detail of a project without ever getting to the point, for the sheer pleasure of manifesting how much they have toiled, sweated, worked.

Raise your hand if you didn't want to shoot yourself a beer drowned in rum, binge on Nutella like there's no tomorrow until you pass out glycemic, or teleport to the loneliest solitary confinement cell in a maximum-security prison while the colleague on duty fuffed on his or her prowess by giving unsolicited and unskilled opinions on what is actually your job.

Minutes and minutes that seem almost like hours, where people who do something else, anything but, really anything else, say their piece about the placement of the accent on the "a" in the storefront sign that, left unfixed, has certainly has affected the sales of a right-handed target audience. Or he expresses his improbable opinion by telling you anecdotes of a past successful and brilliant work experience where none of those present were present and can testify.

Inebriated by the rambling words you understandably lose your sense of discourse, perhaps that of your whole life, and you no longer know where you are and why you are there. You don't know why with a mountain of projects to carry on, you are forced to attend expository sessions that accomplish nothing and risk being detrimental, burdensome, sterile.

Let's face it. Part of you knows how to respond to your doubts and suffering. You try to silence it, but sooner or later it finds its way, grabs the microphone.

It tells you, whether you want it to or not, that you are there to respond to the cravings for control, to the loneliness of that manager who wants company, the social pawn of a micromanagement chessboard where everything you do is viewed under a microscope, taken out of context, vivisected

---

cates how much an employee costs the company per hour.

in a metonymic game of the whole for the part and the part for the whole. It tells you that you are there as a microscopic little piece, a puppet in a game where your time has to justify someone else's salary.

And in that moment you know what there is to know: that meetingitis kills. It kills your free time. It kills your patience. It kills your sanity. It kills your evenings and your weekends. Because in order to do your work, the real work, you have to wait, patient and exhausted, for the meeting day to end and the real work day to begin: the night one, the weekend one where you have to catch up.

Meetingitis is the main reason for work overbooking, for those twelve hours of tireless work a day to meet deadlines.

Meetings, the real ones, the ones you need to move projects forward operationally and tactically, you sometimes do on the sly. With a trusted group of colleagues, fearless comrades for the job, you make arrangements, you mark up a doctor's appointment on Outlook, and you actually do a Teams on project progress and the "Feeding of the Multitude": you track the promotion on Salesforce[101], I do the communication on the site and at the point of sale, you sell the product. Stuff like that. Simple, no?

There is to be said that a little help has been given to us by technology, with that priceless opportunity for concealment that Teams video blocking, Google Meet, Hootsuite, Zoom offer you, with that participate and don't participate that allows you to do other things when meetings are not necessary, not for you at least.

Some call this, no doubt rightly, disrespectful of other people's work, others call for the participants' video screen always on. I call it a matter of otherwise polite survival.

With the transfer of meetings from offline to online, I have

---

101 Alluded to here is CRM, the customer relationship management of the San Francisco-based cloud computing company now listed on the New York Stock Exchange.

personally been able to reclaim twenty, I say twenty minutes of lunch time that I have not taken in decades. Decades of sandwiches in front of the screen, crumbs on the keyboard, blocked digestions, galloping gastritis.

Sometimes I get to thirty minutes and indulge in a little stroll around the man-made quagmire we all affectionately call a lake, a small mirror of stale water populated at times by ducks and mosquitoes overlooked by our headquarters.

The tour of the lake and the friends of the lake, people like me who make their daily rounds before returning to the office, we owe to you, to technology. To the ability to connect remotely, to the magical, magnificent online communication platforms that even in the pandemic era and in total smart working have allowed us to call meetings indefatigably, to engage with colleagues on a daily basis, to keep in touch with each other, to see each other in the evenings for old-fashioned drinks, to recreate the lost sense of community. And black out the videos and zero out the audio and do something else, while live.

At first, as a neophyte, you would just block out the video, hiding behind a black screen, at best with some token, like your initials, or a smiling photo uploaded to the linking platform account, but colleagues would quickly detect the rhythmic clicking of your keyboard. Muting the audio was the solution. The mute button is magic. It is life.

"Forget about it", says Al Pacino in *Donnie Brasco*[102]. Companies around the world have enabled or accelerated work-from-home dynamics.

They call it smart working and smart it really is by enabling managers to manage work in a more flexible and sustainable way.

Only the manager by chance, devoted to working tire-

---

[102] 1997 drama film directed by Mike Newell and starring Johnny Depp and Al Pacino, the story of an undercover FBI agent on the verge of an identity crisis. Sort of what happens to the manager by chance in the company.

lessly and terrified of horror vacui, finds there is nothing smart about it, stupid rather.

You start responding to the first negative comments on social media at 7 a.m., certain that sooner or later in the day you will find a way to get out of your pajamas and take a shower. At 8.30 p.m., your husband finds you still there, fasting, nailed to your study desk, a victim of the PC, meetings, Excel, and doubling projects with fourth flip that the pandemic crisis period has imposed. You are not a nurse, not a doctor, but you spend the day putting Band-Aids on projects gone bad and slipped into the amniotic fluid of the mother of all ills, the crisis.

Yet that very same technology that takes away our hunger and sleep has been the harbinger, for some of us, of a momentous revolution. A courageous and fearless movement, perhaps precisely because they are sheltered in their own homes, to reflect on some of the toxic relationships present in business. In many companies around the world.

The experience, some more than others, we have all experienced it at least once. Energetic colleagues, impulsive colleagues. Anxious colleagues, pretentious colleagues. Colleagues who chase you around the office, break into your projects out of sheer narcissistic necessity and leave. Colleagues you discover, to your amazement, turn off like the light switch if, in a moment of overstepping your bounds - yours and those of your patience - your rusty phalanx inadvertently slips on the red button of the online video chat. "Turn it off".

A revolution? Yes, a revolution. For those who believed until yesterday that relationships with "complex" colleagues could work only with imposing efforts by the more posed of acceptance, transparency and communicative flexibility, discovering that work also proceeds in other relational modes, respectful of oneself and others - who if they lose their temper win the right to oblivion - is a revolution. The pandemic revolution in education.

As if a huge disinfectant went over it and sanitized the environments. Even in business.

The principle of principles remains firm: meetingitis can kill. Before you cross that threshold, before you click the "participate" button, at the very least make sure you can tick off the video function and audio function in case of emergency.

A gesture can save a life.

The Manager Goes to School

I love the air you breathe in graduate classes. They are carefree atmospheres. The lightheartedness of the student, the lightheartedness of possibility. Anticipation marries expectation, doses the charge of notions that are already yesterday's and make you foreshadow a new tomorrow. I love the air you breathe in master's programs, the creative power of a new perspective, the inevitable growth in relationship, the incomparable value of humanity.

A self-respecting manager by chance has been converted from the first time he enters the office to the religion of continuing education. A challenging creed that replaces prayers with tomes of strategic marketing and management engineering manuals, webinars and online in-depth sessions. And refresher newsletters, instructional podcasts, videos of TED talks[103]. Professional enhancement courses, master's degrees, executive masters, double degrees are part of his collection, flaunted like diamond lines on one's resume and worn like trophies on one's LinkedIn page.

You have to be brought to it, but once you're in the loop, it's game over. Like eating cherries or chocolate toffee. One course pulls on another, cleverly mixed with international conferences, IAB[104], Richmond[105] and related, and meetings

---

[103] TED is a platform for sharing talks - ideas worth spreading - and speeches from around the world. TED talks have been run by the U.S.-based private nonprofit organization Sapling Foundation since 1984. The talks are thematically organized and subtitled in many languages. Don't know it? Catch up: www.ted.com.

[104] The international advertising bureau is the most important association in the field of digital advertising worldwide and represents the entire advertising industry. It was founded in 1996 by Randall Rothenberg.

[105] Since 1994 Richmond has organized B2B events and strategic business forums in Milan, London, Basel and New York. The Richmond marketing forum and the Richmond digital marketing forum are two fixtures in the

with the gurus of the moment, from Seth Godin[106] to Michael Porter[107], from Vijay Govindarajan's boxes[108], to Luciano Floridi's *onlife*[109], from philosopher Byung-Chul Han[110] to Simon

    manager by chance's annual event booklet.
106 U.S. marketing guru and entrepreneur, Seth Godin has to his credit such seminal essays as *Purple Cow. Transform Your Business by Being Remarkable* (2002), *Small Is the New Big* (2006) and the more recent *This Is Marketing. You Can't Be Seen Until You Learn to See* (2018). Follow his blog seths.blog, full of interesting insights.
107 An American economist and lecturer at Harvard Business School, he is the author of theories that have permeated the history of marketing, from the analysis of the five competitive forces in a market that are likely to determine a company's fate-direct competitors, suppliers, customers, potential entrants, producers of goods that replace your own-to the valuable concept of the value chain, a model-that of the value chain-that describes the business organization as a set of primary processes and supporting and supply processes.
108 Of Indian descent, Govindarajan is, according to Forbes, "one of the top five most respected executive coaches on Strategy" in the world, professor of International Business at Dartmouth College's Tuck School of Business and founder of Tuck's Center for Global Leadership. Most notable is his innovation-in-execution model of the Three-box solution. For Govindarajan in the market, you are in the first box if you close your gap by aiming for competition and efficiency in the present; you are in the second box if you gain a competitive advantage with a new performance by forgetting the past; you are in the third box if you achieve monopoly by creating new paradigms and reinventing the future of the market. Another popular theory is that of reverse innovation, the last phase of a journey in markets that has taken us from globalization to local innovation via glocalization. In the last phase of reverse innovation, multinational corporations reinvent the market by taking innovations designed for poorer nations and adapting and developing them on a large scale for the rest of the world.
109 Luciano Floridi is full professor of philosophy and ethics of information at Oxford University and director of the Digital Ethics Lab. Since 2020 he has been professor of Sociology of Communication at the University of Bologna. *The Fourth Revolution: How the Infosphere is Reshaping Human Reality* is a 2014 essay where the philosopher details the concept of onlife, whereby factually in everyone's life online and offline constitute an organic, indistinguishable and coexistent continuum.
110 A critic of neoliberalism, the Korean philosopher, a professor of philosophy at the University of Berlin, has to his credit a fruitful output of essays that probe with intellectual honesty, lucidity and rare consistency the thinking that runs through our society. *The Burnout Society, Psychopolitics, The Expulsion of the Other, The Transparency Society, Saving Beauty, In the Swarm, The Agony of Eros, What is Power, The Scent of*

Sinek, that there is no manager left on the face of the earth who does not wear on the ring finger of his left hand his *golden circle*[111], supplanting the wedding ring.

Schools for managers are magical places, populated by people eager to learn new powers, like students at Hogwarts, intent on experimenting with new potions to transform themselves into unbeatable dragons or powerful whales. And they are challenging places.

You attend them in the hours stolen from your free time, thinking about a better future, about how to become an even more capable manager and position yourself in better companies than the one that houses you at that moment in your life. Firmer, more rewarding, more appreciative. And then the sacrifice will be worth it.

You show up on your first day of school with a laptop instead of a briefcase and your career path goals instead of Bic pens, but sharpened just the same.

Ready to write a new page.

Ready to share a life-changing growth path with other managers like you, you tell yourself.

Ready to experience even there, even in school, the same dynamics you find in the company.

Here is the climbing manager, sitting in the front row along with the geeky manager.

Here is Cassandra, forlorn in the back row, next to the Nerd and Penelope, with only one hope in her hands: that at the end of the course someone will finally believe her.

Here's the incontinent manager, who has already pro-

Time, Topology of Violence, The Disappearance of Rituals, The Palliative Society: Pain Today, Non-Things, Infocracy, Vita contemplativa, The crisis of narration: read them, read them all.

111 It was the year 2011 and Simon Sinek published the essay *Start With Why* and captivated fifty-seven million viewers on the TED platform with his *golden circle*, a consumer-centric theory such that people don't buy what you do, they don't buy how you do it but they buy why you do it. Supporting his leadership model is a series of compelling case studies, from Apple to Martin Luther King to the Wright brothers.

fused one of his classic farts in class, horrifying Chanel and Vulcan, who immediately moved three rows over to talk managerial aesthetics and communicative deportment with the designer manager, who knows a lot about it.

Here he is, right in the center of the classroom, the structured manager, a little more strutting than the others, studying the perimeter of his deskmates. It pleases him to have next to him the performance manager and the Highlander manager with whom he will take the final project work, counting on beating out the competition from the enlightened manager.

You often find the Willy Wonka manager at the coffee machine, looking for reassuring sweets and delicacies, in the thick of conversation with the aging manager, who seeks company in his wallflowering.

The manager in love stands by the window and sighs. He has already fallen head over heels for his desk mate. Pontius Pilate washes his hands of her.

The only manager you will never find at these educational gatherings is the Great Dictator. He is managerial. He doesn't need it.

For everyone else there is the guarantee of a new course, a new skill, a new hope. For everyone else there is the air you breathe in continuing education courses. It is the air of possibility.

The Manager's Tools

Nails, hammer, Kalashnikov model AK 101, a set of Japanese Global knives, scimitars, time bombs. And more arsenic without lace[112], lethal ecstasy, acid cocktails and bullets. Potions of invisibility, cloaks of power and mantras of disappearance.

Beneath the blazer the manager by chance has a combat tool kit, invisible to most but not to other managers. Every self-respecting manager possesses one. It acts solely in his mind but, as the wise man says, the important thing is that it works. At least for him.

Metaphorical weapons aside, on a day-to-day basis the tools with which the manager is most familiar are PowerPoint, Excel and the ever-present, affectionate KPI, without which he doesn't even go to bed, only to find them again the next morning, valuable collectors of the night's performance - did I make good love? Did I improve my rem phase compared to the previous day? What percentage did I achieve?-, companions on the journey to the office, evaluators of city traffic and the pace of stair climbing if the manager is a Highlander and does not take the elevator.

The PowerPoint is factually the most abused tool in business but also the most indicative.

In the early 2000s on my third interview as communications and digital marketing manager in a respectable corporation they basically told me that. They had me meet the CEO, a tall guy with arched eyebrows and eyes as piercing as a jackhammer. We entered the BOD room, traditionally developed in length and occupied in the center by a long black table. He sat at the top. I took a seat at the bottom.

---

112 *Arsenic and Old Lace* is a hilarious 1944 film directed by Frank Capra.

We looked straight into each other's eyes without uttering a word. Eventually the CEO took the floor. "Can you do PowerPoints?" he asked.

At the moment I was surprised and incredulous. That role involved far more skills than the mundane use of PowerPoint. Yet in that sentence was encapsulated the corporate aletheia, the real function and at the same time the fate of the manager.

The manager by chance spends his days between meetings and working out complex PowerPoint's with beautiful forms that tangibly and well demonstrate the effectiveness of his work. That same work he himself can't seem to get done, in the scraps of time stolen from continuous meeting sessions on Teams and other ravenous PowerPoints, in need of attention and performance.

He does not in fact know where he finds the time to pursue projects, to organize team work, to actually work for opportunities to build other presentations that that "work" represents him, in line with his real job description. A job within a job, a meta-job where the lion's share is the presentation slides.

The PowerPoint's counterbalance is the shy Excel, which often represents the substance of those PowerPoints, appearing there in dignified tabular form. Among the most frequently used formulas, it is no accident that the VLOOKUP, the function that finds elements in a table or range by row, stands out, and does so by repurposing as a criterion that verticality that is so mirror-like to the corporate organizational chart and the pyramidal tendency that all of us managers, climber manager in pole position, know so well.

Manager Meets other Managers

It sounds like an initiatory rite but it is not. It is much more than that. The meeting of a business manager with managers of other companies follows a very precise protocol, a handbook of tacit rules that must be followed slavishly, under pain of diplomatic disaster between companies.

First and foremost, the introductions. At the beginning of a meeting with managers of unfamiliar companies, agencies, and suppliers, the phantom table round with summary presentation of who we are, what we do in the company, and what we do there with them is standard practice.

This is followed, coveted, by the exchange of business cards in the case of in-person meetings. In deferred meetings on conversational platforms such as Zoom, Teams and Google Meet, the card is replaced with final recap emails to all participants with each person's references attached.

The card moment is - I must admit - my favorite. It is that moment in which we all become a little bit of a child again. Those minutes of convivial exchange where you pass on to each other who you are in miniature, remembering when your desk mate had the Vialli[113] figurine in the Panini collection and did not want to give it to you in exchange for a Gullit[114], which you had double. Little daily fades of times gone by.

There follows the presentation of the projects to be tack-

---
113 One of the best center forwards between the 1980s and 1990s, Gianluca Vialli played for Sampdoria, Juventus, Chelsea and the Italian national team.
114 Dutch footballer Ruud Gullit gained fame in Italy playing as a midfielder and striker for AC Milan from 1987. He is remembered for his dexterity on the field and strictly dreadlocked hair.

led together, and this is where the going gets tough. It is the phase of the meeting in which you have to prove to the other who you are, in a challenge of who is more talkative, in order to win the throne of conductor of the game. A singular tussle somewhat reminiscent of fencing with elegant lunges and subtractions.

The equation changes depending on the number of addendums present. If you are the only one in your company at that particular meeting, then you will take it upon yourself to represent it to the fullest extent. Presumably before the meeting you will have discussed with your boss the course to be taken and the goals to be brought home.

If along with you is another manager from the same company, there are two scenarios on the horizon. In the more mature case, the two managers, who tend to be hostile, will put down the hatchet for the good of the company, showing solidarity and steadfastness in their position.

In the worst of situations, physiological adversity will peep out with impunity, albeit restrained, and risk ridiculing the negotiation.

The principle of all principles remains firm: every meeting has the potential to be a vanity fair, a showdown by showdown, a race to see who can talk over each other the most.

However bitter the confrontation between company A and company B may be, the epigone of the meeting will most likely always be the same: toothy smiles and big packs on the shoulders. An approach that has several nuances.

The subtext "we're friends anyway even though I've haggled the best price, let's go have a drink together" has been alive and well for centuries among males, ever since tribal neighbors stole a few heads of sheep from each other and then tapped beer together.

No problem among women either, with only the substitution of beer for a dry martini, appetizers aside.

The clear pacts and long friendship style wins at gender

parity, but becomes a slippery slope in the case of male-female confrontation. A woman who gets her way with the male is still, in the 21st century, experienced by her counterpart as "aggressive" and undeserving of the olive cocktail.

Obviously, any generalization is undue, but writing this is a woman who has experienced these episodes galore, often in comparison with female managers to whom it has happened just as much. My friends and I may not be statistically significant, but it surely must mean something, don't you think?

Commendations are followed by feedback in the company, a parenthesis of levity where you can at total liberty fleece the administrative manager's dress, challenge the CEO's tie, smile at the salesperson's gaffe.

It is not a moment of great human stature, much less intellectual. It doesn't happen often but it does happen. If we managers did not allow ourselves these freedoms among ourselves, we would periodically risk explosion.

In the game of sides, we know that the managers of Company B are doing the same at this very moment. And so the urge for that beer together rises to let all disagreements slip down the drain and drown judgments and opinions in alcohol.

The Manager and the Consultant

Among the most controversial relationships involving the manager's emotional sphere, the relationships he weaves with third-party professional figures, such as consultants and trainers, stand out, without a shadow of a doubt.

The dynamic is complex.

If it is the manager who has selected the consultant out of a need to complement his or her own skills and improve planning in the company, here the relationship is idyllic.

The consultant, whom for narrative expediency we will call Alexander - an overused name in consulting firms around the world - becomes his best friend, his support in difficult choices in the company. Penelope knows something about this. Penelope loves her Alexanders in the exact same way, as a mother loves her children, as an Oriental prince appreciates every pearl in his harem.

In the unfortunate case that Alexander has been chosen by and imposed on management, that is when the symphony changes. The relationship is played out on a battleground that all of us managers are unfortunately familiar with.

Alexander comes to the company, strong in his consulting role recognized by management, ready to prove his superiority to ordinary management and do his job well. The consultant feels more capable, faster, more experienced. If he were not, they say, management would not have called him in to fix the situation, to put his thousand-euro patches in the company. And most of the time he is right. Some managers really believe that their management is not up to the task, sometimes with good reason, sometimes in total devaluation mode of the professionalism around them.

So that the capable manager is faced with two options.

The first is to engage in an internal struggle to rout Alexander and put him back in his place, a grueling and difficult goal to achieve. In most cases you will find yourself put in a bad light by hostile attitude and inability to confront, boyishly unaware that the consultant does not just "consult". He is the watchful eye of management, evaluator of your performance, detached judge and architect of your business growth.

The second way involves watchful eyes and capitalization on experience. Why not use the consultant in silent alliance to succeed in bringing to management ideas and projects that professed by the manager would have no chance of realization? To succeed requires circumspection and simulation.

It is necessary to learn from Frank Abagnale Jr, the protagonist of *Catch Me If You Can*[115], an artist of fiction and circumvention, who really existed and who, before he was nineteen years old, had managed to make a fortune pretending to be a pilot, a state attorney, and a doctor, eluding the FBI and seducing others.

It is therefore necessary to play proximity with Alexander, with acting, to induce him to take your ideas as his own. And pass them on to management. A trick that is not so difficult.

If the consultant is good and you are equally good, your ideas will naturally converge, and that's it.

If you fall short, there is no Alexander to listen to you, and the demerit is all yours.

In contrast, the convincing process is of easy reach if Alexander is a Glue consultant, a copy-and-paste consultant who

---

[115] *Catch Me If You Can* is a 2002 film directed by Steven Spielberg and inspired by the autobiographical novel of the same name by Frank Abagnale Jr, who defrauded half the world between 1964 and 1969.

is inclined to take in what management reports to him, make it his own, perhaps improve it, and re-propose it as a solution to the Management Board. It goes without saying that the Glue consultant is the favorite of every manager in the world, by chance and otherwise. The manager gets his project materialized, Alexander makes his piggyback, the management confirms the goodness of his choice and the foresight of his intervention.

And they all lived happily ever after and manager.

The Manager Goes to the Dance

There is an infallible test to understand whether you, too, belong by nature to the noble category of manager by chance. As truthful as the truth serums of the James Bond spy movies, as effective as the Spanish Inquisitions, as disruptive as the most moving episode of *The Oprah Winfrey Show*.

Get comfortable, have a drink, sit in your favorite chair and answer these questions:

1. When you get an invitation from management to attend a dinner with the management team you:

a	answer that you would love to but your mother has hemorrhoids and you have to go help her		
	yes	no	probably

b	respond that unfortunately you have lost your voice and could not contribute to the conversation as if anyone had ever allowed you to do so		
	yes	no	probably

c	you become speechless from shock		
	yes	no	probably

d	you pretend to be your answering machine and ask them to leave a message
	yes no probably

2. You love at least three of these items:

a	caviar, even if it gets lodged in your tooth crevice
	yes no probably

b	the most uncomfortable but coolest couture clothes you've ever worn
	yes no probably

c	perpetually wearing wrap-around jackets, even if you had sausage for lunch
	yes no probably

d	experimental jazz that John Cage in comparison is a classic
	yes no probably

e	challenges, i.e., stealing company secrets from the secretary or executive secretary
	yes no probably

f	getting the secretary or management secretary to steal company secrets
	yes no probably

g	effective but sandaper-like toilet paper		
	yes	no	probably

h	open spaces		
	yes	no	probably

i	piped music in convention center restrooms		
	yes	no	probably

l	collecting calls on online platforms as if it were an Olympic relay race		
	yes	no	probably

3. In order to avoid the corporate Christmas party would you swallow a camel alive even if you were a vegetarian?

yes	no	probably

If you answered yes to question 1 and question 3 and did not pass the three affirmative units in question 2, then, my friend, you are one of us. Welcome to the world of managers by chance. Managers by chance, the real ones, abhor corporate social life outside the walls of the company. They fear like a scorpion in the desert conviviality among colleagues. They despise contexts in which you are forced to socialize with people you can barely support during daylight hours. They are afraid of the idea of ending up as a wallflower or, worse, playing the role of scapegoat for the umpteenth time. They hate the idea of trolling for an entire evening with the Sun King's court. They hate that they don't feel comfortable, Calimeri[116] in a henhouse of white feathers.

---

116 In 1963 *Carosello* first introduced to the Italian public the irresistible Calimero, a chick "sponsored" by the Mira Lanza laundry detergent com-

Let's not get them wrong: they too like to have a beer in the company of their colleagues, the good ones. Chatting about themselves and their projects with other managers by chance. Also compare themselves with the Willy Wonkas, the Chanels, the climbers, the Peter Pan's and, why not, managers in love. Managers by chance love direct confrontation, one-on-one sessions, vertical relational insights, were it even with Great Dictators.

What's just not in their wheelhouse is entering workgroup dynamics in private time. The work-private association confuses them, the promiscuity sends them into a tailspin. The manager by chance spends the entire workday focused on the what to be able to emotionally manage the outline, the meetingitis, the Great Dictator, the climber... Getting through the evening safely is his daily goal.

Crossing the threshold of home and being able to be the accidental human being that he is is as liberating as can be for him. But asking him to succeed and wear the mask again on the evening shift, lo and behold, is like telling Sisyphus that he cannot shift the weight he carries on his shoulders for a moment to go pee. It is a cruel gesture.

If you look at it from this perspective, if you conceive of the manager by chance as Dr. Jekyll in a suit and tie who at night becomes Mr. Hyde[117] in pajamas, like a vampire in reverse, refractory to the light of the premises in the presence of his colleagues, here it all comes together, everything is clear to you. The manager by chance is a diurnal animal. He can work even at night, but in total solitude. If you ask him to go out for a glass of wine he does it with those he really likes, with those he is free to be the accidental human being that he is.

---

pany, who had fallen into soot. He was drawn by Nino and Toni Pagot.
117 *The Strange Case of Dr. Jekyll and Mr. Hyde* is an 1886 short story by Robert Louis Stevenson, set in late 19th century Victorian London.

The Manager Reaps Victims

This is an important chapter in the journey of getting to know the animated population that lives in the company.

It is the Manager by Chance part of Corporate Social Responsibility, its social side, the warnings for use.

A manager, even the most harmless one, can hurt his employees, other managers, friends and relatives.

But let's go step by step. The famous saying "The fish stinks from the head"[118] finds a life of its own and a stench in the company. The style and methodology of individual employees, especially junior ones, are somehow deeply influenced by the behavior of the manager of reference.

Prepared, punctual and happy employees will most likely have prepared and punctual managers. Employees who are entropic and non-compliant with company rules will follow the mood of their boss in the company.

Being accurate with a confusing boss is about as painful as you can get. Such an employee will not have an easy life, and in any case his or her path and working mode will be undermined by having as a reference a boss who is unable to appreciate and value that skill because it does not belong to him or her, therefore he does not consider it important.

Thus, it is essential for the manager to be aware of his social responsibility. In quarrels between managers, employees also get in the way, in the construction of a corporate climate that is anything but harmonious and serene, far removed from the principles of Ikigai[119] that are so fashionable

---
118 The manager by chance likes to think that "the fish doesn't stink. Sometimes it smells from the head".
119 Japanese philosophy that defines some simple rules for living a worthy and happy life. In approaching one's mission in the world, Ikigai suggests

in this historical phase. A good manager must try to preserve his team from such compromises.

Here are some useful tips for taking care of your neighbor at yet another improper attack by the usual quarrelsome colleague or the snub of the moment, as the deep and justified desire to beat you up to the point of bloodshed in the hallway creeps through your thoughts and anger rises:
- lock yourself in the nearest bathroom and indulge in five to ten minutes of hypersound muted improperness so that the departments closest to the bathroom does not call for assistance;
- excuse yourself from the office for a moment and take a brisk walk around the block, don't take the elevator on the way back, and take deep, sonorous breaths before the entrance. You'll come back to the office as exhausted as Rocky Balboa after training and you won't have a voice to say Adrian,[120] let alone engage your folks in the event;
- train yourself to stop. Let the fellow Vulcan erupt, and imagine yourself poolside, a strawberry Daiquiri in hand, the wind in your hair, the sun caressing your face. A perfectly skilled Cuban waiter hands you the best snacks you can remember. Nothing matters but yourself and your breath. You will struggle at first but tenacity will help. Equip yourself with a stopwatch to note your performance improvements. At the end of the alignment that stopwatch will disappear into the depths of chlorine;
- look your counterpart in the eye and give him a metaphor-

---

identifying what we like to do, what we know how to do, what we might get paid for, and what the world needs. The convergence of the answers allows us to identify our personal mission. If you want to go deeper, I recommend the book *The Little Book of Ikigai: Live a happy and long life the Japanese way* by Ken Mogi, a Japanese scientist, researcher at Sony Computer Science Laboratories and professor at the Tokyo Institute of Technology. The translation of Ikigai is "reason for being".

120 "Adrian" is the shout of joy proclaimed by boxer Rocky Balboa in the 1976 film *Rocky* directed by John G. Avildsen and starring Sylvester Stallone. The feature film, which racked up three Academy Awards, was followed by five more films and two spin-offs.

ical punch in the nose. You see the metaphorical blood splash and a smile appears on your face. It is a real smile. You are a fully satisfied manager. Sometimes it helps to see your counterpart in his underwear;
- you leave the room and don't return. An extreme but extremely effective solution. If you are not a wizard of assertiveness, you can always simulate an illness, a sudden visit to the dentist, your wife's delivery even if you are not married.

All of these tips will help you get back to your Ikigai, to the principles of Eastern philosophy applied to everyday life that will make you a happy manager and your team a steadfast and serene team. Ikigai recommends starting with the little things, appreciating them, forgetting yourself, focusing on the here and now, and living in as harmonious and serene an environment as possible. Little pills of wisdom that should be preserved in your daily life, work and family.

Raise your hand if in the midst of a protracted meeting you have not felt terrible guilt toward your family, your partner or companion and your children and pets.

"What am I going to tell Rufus when I get home...?" is the thought that hovers between slides, as if the company has become our secret lover, to whom we give the time we should devote to our loved ones.

Step forward for those who always know how to justify yet another weekend in front of the PC, while the children squeal in the other room. A widespread sentiment in the managerial population, especially for women.

I know wonderful managers frustrated by not being present mothers, smart working managers ankylosed by the family management of online school and work, wives and husbands furious at their partners' lack of attention with their heads perpetually on a project that is not their own.

Widespread situations, litmus test of a conception of

work as an existential vacuum cleaner, huge blotting paper of our lives, eraser that sweeps the boundaries between private and professional, empowered in the pandemic era by at-home work arrangements that increasingly jeopardize, at least for the managerial class, our work life balance.

The manager by chance devourer of Byuan-Chun Hang's essays to the extent that he is now almond-eyed, knows he is living in the midst of a crisis of the neoliberal system. He feels perceptibly that our society of transparency and social media is a society of fatigue, centrifuged by a continuous self-burning of our selves toward the best performance, the best performance. A self-induced diktat of perfection that leads to exhaustion.

He also knows that in the midst of the storm he has little room for action. He can cultivate in his own little garden attention to small things and the common good and hope that others will epidemically do the same, dreaming of an enlightened, human- and child-friendly capitalism.

PILLS

How to Survive

It goes without saying that the people of managers constitutionally need to find contrivances that will get them through the day, the week, the month, the year as painlessly as possible.

There is no single solution, no common key. There are clues, success stories, tactical approaches and pills of wisdom stacked empirically like bricks that one on top of the other make up the manager's protective front by accident, his Canadian tent, the Kalashnikov spitting flowers and smiling at the world.

Here then, in no particular order, are our saving pills, our how-tos for managing the present and looking to the future with the optimism and insight that only a manager by chance can have sharpened over the years.

Call them contrivances, trivial suggestions that are not meant to be nor can they be all-encompassing solutions but diversions that allow you to acquire some breathing time before the arrival of a new storm.

#violence1
What to do if a coworker verbally assaults you in person
Fake a sudden loss of hearing to the point of exhaustion of the interlocutor who, dissatisfied with the lack of response, will leave the room and the combative intent.

Also approved is the rat face with prominent muzzle and fixed gaze without manifesting any emotion. Remain there, impassive as a stockfish watching the agitated one like a meteor watches a passing black hole.

Plausible alternatives include a sudden migraine, a tooth abscess, or the obviously simulated call of your mother suffering from sciatica in her right arm.

Talking back is not ruled out, although - it pains me to report it for scientific rigor - the margin of probability of success is not very high. In those moments the furious manager is blinded by anger and seeks a way to vent his human "inappropriateness". Sometimes a measured and decisive stop succeeds, sometimes it makes things far worse.

The question to ask is always the same. Is it really worth it? Does verbally telling him to fuck off make me a better human being and resolve the situation? It doesn't hurt to try, althought it would be better to succeed.

#violence2
What to do if a colleague verbally assaults you via Teams
The answer can be found in the chapter "Meetingitis Kills. Read the warnings carefully", which I highly recommend you reread carefully. Sliding your little finger over the red "turn off" button on the current chat is highly recommended.

Alternatively, the provisions for direct live verbal aggression apply, with the only variation being the protective screen that stands between you and the interlocutor.
Other possible suggestions via chat include a technical glitch, a dropped line, the ringing of the Amazon courier at your doorstep even though you are in the office at the time, an appendicitis attack, a telegram from Brad Pitt asking you to join him in New York City.

#violence3
What to do if a colleague verbally assaults you via email
The mood is always. Don't respond. Never. Make Kronos[121] one of your best friends and wait at least twenty-four hours before any clarification vis à vis.

If the wait weighs you down and the urge to respond is at the touch of a button, step away from your desk. Take a walk, oxygenate your brain, perform a jog on the spot, drag your-

---

121 In Greek mythology Kronos is master of time, titan and father of Zeus.

self over the vending machine and shoot a KitKat, such as it is, whole, down your esophagus, or shred it with your incisors at the speed of light, the way a Japanese fisherman shreds seaweed every morning with a thin, very very thin blade.

Alternatively, take a piece of paper and jot down everything you would like to say to your colleague. Improper remarks, insults, wishes for epidermis disfiguring but still momentary and non-life-threatening diseases, genitalia falling off like leaves in autumn, punches on the nose complete with blood splatters scattered all over the face and shirt, and whatever worse your anger can imagine.

Reread it all with cautious attention, as a foodie, immediately after placing an order at a starred restaurant, rereads the menu to confirm to himself his choice, with the satisfaction of foretasting a dish beyond his daily reach. Now gently deposit your menu in the wastepaper basket after diligently shredding it.

Apply the principles of quantum physics and imagine every cell in your body projected to the next day, each lying and composed on a verdant meadow populated with daisies, on the bank of a cool stream. Feel the sun caressing your face, the bees buzzing industriously, the birds happy. Chase away the thoughts of death that burst from time to time into the sky of your idyllic picture as the north wind drives away storm clouds.

If the task does not sufficiently satisfy you, repeat it until lunch break arrives, a precious opportunity to get up and re-select some rosemary crackers from the usual machine in the relaxation area.

You will have blown the morning but by then the worst will be over.

#idiocy
What to do if your boss is an idiot
The well-known Spanish singer Jarabe de Palo said it: it

depends.[122] It depends on the degree of dumbness and the nature of the dumbness itself.

In the face of a harmless goof, devoid of intent and without consequence, the best possible attitude is disregard, acceptance, even affection. The risk is that of role override and usurpation of the throne on behalf of others, but it is a contained risk if that goof even likes everyone in the end. To bad you will get a new, much less dumb, even capable boss.

Aggressive and hurtful dumbness, on the other hand, deserves an array formation, in a Spartan phalanx . You can try to be assertive, you can try to pretend you don't understand, you can even spend your working hours glossing over how molasses slips on the pancake or Carolina Kostner[123] on the ice rink, but you will struggle to tick it off. Ignorance is the source of all evil.

If you believe in progress and reincarnation, you can hope for better chances at *prochaine fois*.

If you are an optimist by nature or exercise, you can fit into the corporate mobility program by aiming for a happier function.

If you are equipped with a healthy capacity for dialogue with reality, you can look around and put yourself back in the marketplace, capitalizing on recent experience. In the next company, you tell yourself, you will spot from the first approaches a possible dumb boss, tending to be incompetent, tending to be egotistical, tending to be susceptible to criticism, tending to be averse to freedom of speech and expression, suffering from pawing micromanageriality, the inconsistent and annoying giggling, low-shouldered posture and

---

122 *Depende* is a song by Jarabe de Palo that raged on the charts in 2012. "Depending on how you look at it, everything depends" is one of the stanzas of the song, extolling a gnoseological relativism that finds agreement among managers by chance all over the world.

123 A nine-time Italian champion and world champion in 2012, this iceskater from Bolzano has racked up a substantial number of awards over her successful career. If she were a manager, she would definitely be a Nerd in her field.

pelvis mellifluously thrust forward, to cleave the air and embrace the world. You'll recognize it right away, you tell yourself, and you'll watch out for it, you repeat, lying to yourself. Perhaps you will become friends with it, blinded by the presumption that it is so easy to be smarter than a dumb boss. Perhaps you will be able to disguise your intelligence and go unnoticed.

In fact, nature always takes its course. In the end, there is only one person who can handle a bad dumb boss: another dumb boss. If you can, ask yourself a few questions. In fact, don't. Being dumb is sometimes a choice.

#dictatorship
What to do if your boss is a dictator

If you have done your homework and studied the chapter "The Dictator Manager" thoroughly, you know for a fact how hardly immovable the stature of the Great Dictator is for a single, small, scattered manager.

However, history teaches us that great dictatorships have been nicked by great collective revolutions. If you are a manager with balls and exasperation in the company hovers supreme, perceive the possibility of a *coup d'état*, a proper downsizing of the Dictator, at your hand and shrewdness.

Ban violence. We are taught this by the great pacifists of the last century, the Martin Luther Kings, the Gandhis and the Nelson Mandelas, defenders of human rights: you don't need the guillotine to change the course of history. You don't need to dirty your hands, you don't need to hymn the guns. It takes lucidity and ingenuity for the sake of the corporate community, for the future of the people of managers. It takes "I have a dream"[124] and proper and substantive planning, a program with content to rebuild the foundations of our society.

---

124 On August 28, Martin Luther King Jr. began his speech at the Lincoln Memorial in Washington, D.C. at a protest march for civil rights, jobs and freedom.

"Great Dictator, your time is over in the recycling bin" we must all say together, water gun in hand. That's where climate change will end, the ozone hole will close and plastic will disappear from the ocean floor. After you are gone, dear Dictator, the spirit of humanity will shine again. And Tom Hardy[125] will ask Cassandra out. And the climbing manager will decide to abdicate the summit.

While waiting for this happy moment, which may never come except at the movies, surround yourself with allies to avoid evil parades and try to pick the right square to stake out.

The Great Dictator constitutionally has no time, ability or willingness to acknowledge your existence. He quickly stigmatizes you on the basis of the first hasty clues, ascribing to you an epithet that will most likely last forever. You might as well from the outset construct the best epithet for him to attribute to you by being very careful in your first interlocutions with him.

Whatever contrivance you find, you should still know that the climate in dictatorship is not the happiest and also triggers in other bystanders corrosive feelings and undignified tactics devoted to the salvation of the individual. A battle of the have-nots.

The Great Dictator will always and everywhere try to undermine your self-esteem, subdue your judgment, publicly humiliate your person and discredit your work. For pure ego pleasure. For pure self-assertion. Not out of annoyance with you. To prove it he would have to acknowledge your existence and deplete it of its usefulness in making him shine.

Then there are the extreme gestures, with their attendant risks. You can opt for Oliviero Toscani-like[126] actions with

---

[125] In the splendid feature film *Locke*, directed by Steven Knight, shot in real time over eight consecutive nights and entirely set inside a car, the British actor plays a site manager grappling with the birth of his son, who was conceived during a night of passion with a woman he met on a work trip.

[126] Great Italian photographer with bold and controversial advertising campaigns. You may remember the 1991 Benetton campaign that immortalized a priest's impudent kiss with a nun.

strong symbolism, such as lying supine on the table in the BOD room, arms folded across your chest, eyes closed, and loudly proclaiming, "She is killing us this way".

You can respond in tone to the Great Dictator with enormous expenditure of energy and risk of being tossed out the window.

You can organize a sit-in at the switchboard and discover yourself sitting on the floor alone while others are immovable at their desks, eyes down to the keyboard and metaphorical whistling.

You can embark on the legal climb, with union reps or lawyers in tow, expending considerable energy.

You can punch them in the nose and end up in jail.

Consider yourself free; you can act as you see fit.

Behind bars, you may ask yourself, "Was it really worth it?" In some cases, the answer may surprise you. It might be "yes".

#affair1
What to do if your boss bangs your colleague or someone of similar rank

If in the chapter "The manager in love" we amiably disquisitioned how complicated love affairs were in the company, here is the right opportunity to talk about the difficult fate of those who do not live that love affair but suffer it. The desk neighbors, the desk mates, the other managers.

If your boss infracts with one or another of your colleagues, be prepared for a time of possible unfairness. And do it with a light heart. Love is blind. The person involved in the affair and his or her entourage of cronies will most likely have the best salary, the best position, the best benefits, the best project assignments. And even if not, that is what you will think, conditioned by a love that does not include you.

One chance to advance your career is to re-enter the entourage of the beloved with the risk that then the love fortunes will change and you will find yourself among the depreciated in the power quotations. A dangerous game. You might as well sit still, do your own thing, and wait.

As much as this state of affairs outrages you there is nothing else you can do.

It rarely helps you to go to the human resources manager who holds a lower position in the organizational chart than your boss, and it does not help you to speak directly to your manager with an open heart because his heart is elsewhere.

Get over it and accept the disruptive power of love with a smile.

#affair2
What to do if you fall in love at the office

This pill is dedicated to the naive, to the dreamers, to those who have not carefully read the chapter "The manager in love", to those who believe in the irresistibility of love and do not imagine that its power can be reversed, that it can come down on you and sweep you away, like an autumn leaf in the gutter.

To them I write that love is a wonderful thing, even more beautiful and easier when consummated outside the corporate walls. Love in the company, developed vertically, acquires the connotations of power that we eviscerated in the previous pills.

If you believe in that love, you know that the only thing to do is to change offices, dissimulate your feelings in public, play discretion.

#stinkers
What to do if one of your co-workers is a stinker

I have been very fortunate in my life as a manager by chance, surrounded by capable and dedicated co-workers, carefully chosen in the selection phase for their skills and their attitude of participation and mutual respect.

Many of them continue to be part of my life even though they go back several companies. Encountering each other is one of the most enriching parts of our existence as earthlings. To cherish those encounters in our memory and make the best of them is a privilege we have.

Only once have I come across a stinker of a co-worker who tended to smile at me as he tried to sober up the other members of the work group and elbow his way into a place in the sun that, had he been patient, he would have gotten anyway on merit because he was good at it.

I am sure he was not fully aware of his ambitious nature. I did nothing to stop him, a little distressed by what I was seeing and by my failure as a leader, a little aware that doing something meant increasing the power of his act.

I kept my role as manager consistent and focused on doing. Then I took him aside and talked to him, without much success. I could not dampen even for a split second his everlasting smile and see what was behind it.

I don't know how to treat a stinking collaborator. What you have to ask yourself is what makes a stinker a collaborator and whether you, as a manager, are able to help him give his best and not his worst.

#overload
What to do if the workload crushes you

This is the leitmotif of the manager by chance. And the solutions are many.

Increase your ability to delegate, play the game of prioritization and organization, raise your hand and ask for help, invite your boss to delegate less, kill the less compelling and useful projects, hire new staff.

If all these solutions turn out to be impractical, then it means you are in an unstructured, understaffed, and in wide probability shrinking business, where you do not have enough budget to hire new staff and all ongoing projects are aimed at the subsistence of the business. In that case, let me tell you, you're screwed.

But don't get overwhelmed by events. After the first few

months, maybe years of sacrifice, remember that working tirelessly twelve hours a day will lead you to exhaustion, to the loss of reason, and your profile will get closer and closer to that of the incontinent manager or Vulcan manager.

The solution lies within you. Set yourself limits, set your alarm clock at for 7p.m., create appointments after work, train yourself to pen drop, and make sure that your non-stop work trip, terribly facilitated by smart working, finds its end where your mental and physical health begins.

If you can't do it, check out our Facebook group of workaholics, good people who want to get out of this insane addiction. Our motto, our claim, our call to action is "Get a life".

#paralysis
What to do if you never get a promotion in the company

I don't want to appear overly Cartesian, but to identify the correct solution we must necessarily appeal to the principle of cause-and-effect. What leads your bosses not to give you a promotion? The answers are many, from your alleged ineptitude to the boss's fear of being outclassed to the economic impossibility of creating a path for you. Having identified the real motivation, you will have no choice but to act.

If you are inept, question yourself and study.

If you are not but your boss thinks you are, prove to him that you are not.

If your boss does not want to make room for you, find another one.

If the company flounders in a difficult situation, you have two options: hold out and wait for better times or abandon ship to sail to safer shores. The manager by chance is unlikely to opt for the second path. He does not like to leave a trail of felonies behind him and loves challenges and supportive work. He will stay, true to the meritocratic credo and confident in the strength of the team.

#awareness
What to do when you discover you're a manager by chance

By now you have swallowed your red pill. Morpheus warned you.[127] You can try escaping, dabbling in crank, throwing yourself into alcohol, crying into the night. You can try to deny your random nature. Start a therapeutic course of regression or rely on the macumba of an exorcist. You will still and always remain a manager by chance.

After an understandable initial phase of absolute, stubborn reticence, joyfully embrace your destiny.

Track down your random brothers, invite them to a company brunch, share with them the nuances of a glorious and numerous lineage, outline a new future of ecumenical and universal randomness. Start a Facebook group, a LinkedIn page, a blog of pure managerial randomness.

Once you get past the first embarrassment you will discover that you are not alone. You will realize that there are many of us. The glorious people of managers by chance. Solidary, happy, aware. Able to found a new humanity.

Like William Adam and Laura Roslin in search of the thirteenth colony, conquering planet Earth.[128] Like the men who one day in the not too distant future will land on Mars to secure a better future for themselves.

---

[127] In the first film of the *Matrix* trilogy Morpheus invites the protagonist Neo to choose between the red pill and the blue pill. "This is your last chance. After this, there is no turning back" Morpheus explains "You take the blue pill - the story ends, you wake up in your bed and believe whatever you want to believe. You take the red pill - you stay in Wonderland and I show you how deep the rabbit hole goes".

[128] This is the concept of the successful sci-fi series *Battlestar Galactica*.

THE DISCIPLE

The Manager Happens to be a Manager

Having reached the end of our roundup of managers by chance and otherwise, there comes the inescapable realization: the manager by chance is also a manager. Whether he wants to be or not.

There is a bit of Cassandra in him. A little bit of Pontius Pilate, if circumstance permits, a dash of Nerd, when analysis looms, and a hefty dose of performance manager. He is Highlander in late-night sessions to close a project, he is climber when he intercepts the needs of power, he is Willy Wonka in search of consolation, and he is, at times, manager in love. In him peeps the designer when it comes to launching a new campaign and in some cases, under stress, he also plays the Vulcan.

In his blood runs some particles of Dictator, which he tries to stifle for lack of alternatives. He not infrequently finds himself structured, gazing, doggedly, at the moves of the other squares. He dreams of being more and more enlightened while the Penelope in him unravels his canvas.

The manager by chance is manager. The manager by chance is.

Let us love him. It is who we are.

And You, Which Manager Are You?

Find out in this test which manager you come close to

Sit comfortably in a chair, not necessarily a recliner, take a deep breath and answer the following questions off the top of your head.

1.	On weekdays, are you happy to get up in the morning?
a	It's none of your business
b	Did anyone notice that I got up?
c	The alarm clock is on time at seven in the morning
d	I don't understand the question
e	What do you mean? It is my duty

2.	What do you love about your work in the company?
a	Always being right
b	The work
c	The KPI
d	The lunch breaks
e	Seeing harmony around me and that things are working

3.	What do you do if your boss blocks a project?
a	Who?
b	I seek a dialogue with him to understand why and possibly make changes that are most helpful to the company and the achievement of goals
c	We evaluated the data together. We agree with him and aim for more

d	He is definitely right
e	The "how" makes a difference. How were you dressed that day?
4.	**It is your first day at work. What are you wearing?**
a	A garment that highlights my figure as an unquestioned leader
b	Simple and harmonious garments. I don't want to be conspicuous
c	My usual outfit
d	With a formal look, I don't go wrong
e	I am what I wear

5.	**Which food appears most frequently on your menu?**
a	Spicy meat
b	Vegetable creams
c	Pre-cooked foods
d	I eat what you eat
e	Mediterranean and balanced foods

6.	**Your favorite movie?**
a	*Touch of Evil*
b	*Fried green tomatoes*
c	*Blade Runner*
d	*The Devil Wears Prada*
e	*The Tree of Life*

7.	**If the blue-haired fairy came and gave you a wish, what would you want?**
a	Everything
b	Equalization of the sexes and world peace

c	Seventy-two hour days
d	Non-stop vacations
e	Nothing more and nothing less than what I have now

8.	If you were a famous person, who would you be?
a	God
b	Joan of Arc
c	Elon Musk
d	The richest man in the world
e	I like the idea of being myself

9.	Which company would you like to work for?
a	My own
b	A non-profit organization with the planet at heart
c	Google
d	I wouldn't want to work
e	An innovative company with the common good at heart

10.	Do you feel like a manager by any chance?
a	How dare you
b	Certainly
c	I need to evaluate the growth trend before answering
d	Mmm...come on, let's have a snack
e	Randomness is not part of my existence

■ **If there is a prevalence of a) answers**
You undoubtedly belong to the family of "matches", a facinorous and caliente population that sees the Dic-

tator manager, the incontinent manager, and the Vulcan manager excel. If you do not admit to this definition, your profile certainly fits the Dictator. If you have a strong artistic streak, you are Vulcan, and if you are farting, well...

■ **If there is a prevalence of b) answers**
You are a "matchstick maker". A manager who tends to be a wallflower in spite of himself. To this category belong full-fledged Cassandras, aging managers, Penelopes and Mary Poppins. Look at it from this perspective: you are not alone. And one day history will prove you right. Someday.

■ **If there is a prevalence of c) answers**
You have a good chance of belonging to the category of "technocrats", little soldiers enlisted in the corporate world as the analytical manager, the Highlander manager, the performance manager, the geeky manager, and the structured manager, who, you know, prefers squares to rounds. You like rules, you like working late into the night, you are crazy about numbers and data.

■ **If there is a prevalence of d) answers**
There is no doubt about it, you are in the group of the "suspended", the managers who live in a limbo of self-induced or purely random non-positioning, where they dream of golden places, vacations together, lack of sweat and other amenities. Here you find all the Pontius Pilates, Peter Pans, Willy Wonkas, climbers and lovers. The great thing about this category is the playfulness and the ability to get along highly with each other, united, all in all, by the dream of doing sweet nothing.

■ **If there is a prevalence of e) answers**
Congratulations. You hold the podium of "elitists"

along with Chanel managers, designers and the enlightened. You are always right in the right place at the right time. And you like yourself the way you are. I struggle to tell you more, a little intimidated by your figure. I invite you to reread the chapters we have devoted to you and to write to me in case you would like to complete the sketches with details I have missed.

Whoever you are, remember. No test can really define who you are. If you have come to this page spontaneously, of your own volition and without skipping chapters, you have only a wide chance of being, like many of us, a manager by chance. Be proud of it.

Acknowledgements

Manager by Chance *is not a lonely path, it is a journey made up of encounters, exchanges and comparisons without which I would not have arrived at this page.*

Thanks to the friends whose reading made a difference, to the people of Manager by Chance *and to all the people who support our project of managerial humanism.*

Thanks to "brother" Sandro Crisafi, who turned the philosophy behind Manager by Chance *into images and a cover, and to my friend Daniela Tudisca, official and not photographer by chance.*

Thank you to my colleagues of today, with whom I take an extra step of manageriality and humanity every day, and thank you to all the managers I have met. I have learned something from each of you.

Thanks to my parents and my brother who, with their trust, helped me to become a manager by chance.

Thanks to the publisher Mauro Morellini who believed in this project and thanks to his incredible staff.

My most heartfelt thanks to Eros, my husband, without whose love and support I would be just a "by chance" wandering randomly in a random universe.

Author

Angela Deganis

Marketing and communication strategist, journalist and speaker, has been planning and managing strategic marketing, digital marketing and communication projects in companies for almost twenty years.

On LinkedIn she has the blog "Vita da Manager", which specializes in management, philosophy in and around the company, and acts as counterpart to her Instagram page @vita_da_manager and disseminates the culture of respect through seminars on social sustainability in the workplace at organizations and institutions.

She has worked with Mondadori Education, Mimesis, Settimo Sigillo, Franco Angeli and De Bastiani as an editor and author and has a background as a press office and agency copywriter. As a journalist, she has worked with Italian newspapers "Corriere della sera" and "Il Gazzettino".

For two years she worked in theater as a prompter and assistant director with Nanni Garella and Michele Placido.

Today Angela is a manager. She loves laughter, the sea, sunshine and daisies.

You can contact her at managerpercaso@gmail.com. She will gladly reply to you in the night time slot.